MADE TO BE
A
WARRIOR

~~~~~~
~~~~~~

by

Phil and Bobi Naukam

Verses marked AMP are scripture quotations taken from THE AMPLIFIED BIBLE, copyright 1954, 1958, 1962, 1964, 1965, 1987 by The Lockman Foundation. All rights reserved. Used by permission. (www.Lockman.org)

Verses marked MSG are scripture quotations taken from THE MESSAGE, Copyright 1993, 1994, 1995, 1996, 2000, 2001, 2002. Used by permission of NavPress Publishing Group.

Verses marked NIV are scripture quotations taken from the HOLY BIBLE, NEW INTERNATIONAL VERSION. Copyright 1973, 1978, 1984, International Bible Society. Used by permission of Zondervan Publishing House. All rights reserved.

Dictionary definitions are from Webster's New Twentieth Century Dictionary, Second Edition. Copyright 1979 by William Collins Publishers, Inc.

To order additional copies of this resource: Contact What If? Freedom Ministries.

ONLINE: www.whatifministries.com
WRITE: PO Box 470252, Tulsa, OK 74147-0252
PHONE: (918) 809.0469

Cover Design by Jeff Burritt, Skip3.com

What If? Freedom Ministries ~ P.O. Box 470252 ~ Tulsa, Oklahoma 74147-0252 ~ 918-249-FREE (3733) ~ www.whatifministires.com

2

INDEX

What If? Freedom Ministries ~ P.O. Box 470252 ~ Tulsa, Oklahoma 74147-0252 ~ 918-249-FREE (3733) ~ www.whatifministires.com

INTRODUCTION

Welcome to boot camp. *Made To Be a Warrior* is your handbook for battle. Our prayer is that this manual will prepare you to fight the good fight better than you have before. You are in a war whether you realize it or not. You can pretend this does not affect you, or you can fight. To fight is better. To fight effectively is better yet.

To gain the most from this study, we have some suggestions.

- Try to spend a little time each day studying the handbook.
- Each chapter ends with scriptures to research, a memory verse, and thinking points. Complete as many as you can, but do not feel compelled to fill each space. Answer what is relevant to you.
- Keep your Bible next to you for reference. You may want to use various translations.
- A concordance and Bible dictionary can be helpful.
- Be honest with yourself as you go through each chapter.
- Take your time. There is no time limit to complete the course.
- Be prepared to discuss the chapter at your small group.
- Pray and ask God to show you the areas of your life that He wants to improve.

We pray that your mind and heart will be changed by the living God as you study *Made To Be a Warrior*. Open yourself to the Holy Spirit, study diligently, and continue to implement what you learn after completing boot camp. May the Lord God Almighty, your Commander-in-Chief, speak His Truth to you in a new way as you prepare to be the Mighty Warrior that God created you to be.

What If? Freedom Ministries ~ P.O. Box 470252 ~ Tulsa, Oklahoma 74147-0252 ~ 918-249-FREE (3733) ~ www.whatifministires.com

4

CALL TO WAR

Psalm 27
A Psalm of David

The Lord is my light and my salvation – whom shall I fear?
The Lord is the stronghold of my life – of whom shall I be afraid?
When evil men advance against me to devour my flesh,
when my enemies and my foes attack me, they will stumble and fall.
Though an army besiege me, my heart will not fear;
Though war break out against me, even then will I be confident.
One thing I ask of the Lord, this is what I seek:
That I may dwell in the house of the Lord all the days of my life,
To gaze upon the beauty of the Lord and to seek him in his temple.
For in the day of trouble he will keep me safe in his dwelling;
He will hide me in the shelter of his tabernacle and set me high upon a rock.
Then my head will be exalted above the enemies who surround me;
At his tabernacle will I sacrifice with shouts of joy;
I will sing and make music to the Lord.
Hear my voice when I call, O Lord; be merciful to me and answer me.
My heart says of you, "Seek his face!" Your face, Lord, I will seek.
Do not hide your face from me, do not turn your servant away in anger;
You have been my helper.
Do not reject me or forsake me, O God my Savior.
Though my father and mother forsake me, the Lord will receive me.
Teach me your way,
O Lord; lead me in a straight path because of my oppressors.
Do not turn me over to the desire of my foes,
For false witnesses rise up against me, breathing out violence.
I am still confident of this:
I will see the goodness of the Lord in the land of the living.
Wait for the Lord; be strong and take heart and wait for the Lord.

What If? Freedom Ministries ~ P.O. Box 470252 ~ Tulsa, Oklahoma 74147-0252 ~ 918-249-FREE (3733) ~ www.whatifministires.com

5

THE MIGHTY WARRIOR CODE OF ETHICS

The Mighty Warrior Code of Ethics is a statement of who and what you are in God's Army. The Warrior Code describes character traits and principles of conduct necessary for soldiers and those who support them.

W   **Winning Attitude**
WARRIORS willingly work hard, do their best at all times, strive to improve daily, and keep Christ first in their lives.

A   **Availability**
God gives WARRIORS the ability to do all things through Christ. WARRIORS make themselves available to do whatever God asks.

R   **Righteousness**
WARRIORS are the righteousness of God in Christ Jesus. They do what is right because it is the right thing to do. They present themselves as authentic, just, upright, and excellent in every situation.

R   **Reliability**
WARRIORS put God's mission first. They are always ready to accept the challenges, risks, opportunities, and excitement of what is set before them. They do whatever it takes to complete the mission.

I   **Integrity**
WARRIORS lead with courage, sound moral principle, and honesty. They know that leadership depends on the trust of those who follow. A WARRIOR's word is his bond.

O   **Obedience**
WARRIORS submit to, honor, and respect those in authority, yield willingly to orders, and perform what is required to achieve victory. WARRIORS abstain from what is forbidden.

R   **Responsibility**
WARRIORS distinguish between right and wrong, accept personal responsibility for their behavior, and aim to be the best of the best. They know that Christ's Freedom requires vigilance, sacrifice, personal commitment, and a WARRIOR spirit that makes the WARRIOR's life unique.

What If? Freedom Ministries ~ P.O. Box 470252 ~ Tulsa, Oklahoma 74147-0252 ~ 918-249-FREE (3733) ~ www.whatifministires.com

6

CHAPTER 1
The Battleground – Your Mind

You are an amazing person. God made you just the way you are with each of your strengths and weaknesses. He did not make a mistake when He created you but made you with a wonderful purpose and plan to accomplish while you are here on this planet we call Earth. God designed you to be a mighty man of honor, a person who demonstrates courage, fearlessness, and bravery, especially in battle. It is never too early or too late to begin that journey of building your character. Don't focus on the past or your weaknesses. You have an awesome future ahead of you no matter where you are in your life now. God loves you, yes, YOU! He wants to forgive and lead you into the adventure of your life. Are you ready? You are a Mighty Warrior. You have been chosen by God to take part in this battle and to win. God is for you and has placed angels and people around you to help you win this war. You are that important to God, your parents, your youth leaders, your pastors, your teachers, and your friends.

During the next several weeks, we hope you catch the vision that God has for you. His love and plan are free, but it will take a lot of work on your part. But we know that you have boundless energy and drive when you know that what you are pursuing is worth the effort. This journey will change your life and teach you how to focus on your Creator and the wonderful things He has in store for you. All you have to do is enter with an open mind and be willing to listen for His voice and obey. Sometimes that will be easy, and other times that will be very difficult. God trusts you so much that He is willing to take a chance on you to be able to fight the battles and ultimately win the war for your heart and well-being. As you progress through this study, put reasoning aside. Don't try to figure out everything. Just be willing to listen to the voice of the Holy Spirit through scripture, prayer, worship, and discussion.

To win the war, you will need to revise some of your thinking patterns and previous ideas. You cannot just wish to change your thinking; you must actively replace your incorrect thoughts with new information consistently. Are you willing to change your way of thinking to line up with the Word of God? The heart cry of God is to bless you and love you just the way you are. Isaiah 1:19 (AMP) says, "If you are willing and obedient, you shall eat the good of the land." Your part is to be willing, and then He will make you able to obey. It is that simple. Yet we tend to make it so complicated.

Two important concepts are critical in this battle – the way you see God and the way you see yourself. How do you see God? Is He a bully in the sky whose goal is to make your life miserable, or is He a loving Father who is firm yet fair in discipline? You may know scriptures **about** God loving you, but do you **believe** that God is your loving Father Who has only your best interests at heart? Many think The Bible teaches that you should fear God, that is, you should be afraid of Him. That is a misinterpretation of the word "fear." The fear of God is a reverent and worshipful fear, an awe of His majesty and power. God does not want you to be afraid of what He might do. On the contrary, He desires you to view Him with awe and respect. Just think, the Creator of the universe loves you, knows you by name, and designed a great plan for your life! Visualize God according to The

What If? Freedom Ministries ~ P.O. Box 470252 ~ Tulsa, Oklahoma 74147-0252 ~ 918-249-FREE (3733) ~ www.whatifministires.com

7

Word. If this is difficult for you, search the scriptures for verses that reinforce God's Truth so your picture of God is accurate according to The Bible and not your background, what other people say, or what you have thought previously. Perhaps you have thought of God as the big Rule Maker whose goal in your life is to ambush you and catch you doing something bad so He can punish you. What if God has given you rules only as a form of love and a way to help you? God's rules are for your benefit and protection. What if He has established boundaries so that He can put you and keep you in a place of blessing?

The other major front in your battle is how you think about yourself. Whether you see yourself as no good and unworthy of love and respect or you come across as macho man, you must have a clear picture of how God sees you. He knows everything about you and still loves you completely and unconditionally. Nothing you can do, think, or say will ever make Him love you any less or any more than He does right now. You may have done some really stupid things in your past. You might think you are not good enough for God to love. You would be wrong! Stop that kind of thinking! God looks at your heart and sees a mighty man of character created in His image. **See yourself the way God sees you!** Remember, God made adolescence. Jesus experienced puberty while on Earth. God understands the struggles of this time in your life.

During the teen years, you are in a constant state of change. Even good change is stressful. Your world may seem confusing, frightening, and unfair; but these years can also be an awesome time in your life. Do not allow the devil to convince you that you have to be rebellious or try things that you know are bad for you. What if God has planned only good for you? What if Satan wants to divert your focus to entice you to follow his evil plans? You are an intelligent young man who would not deliberately make bad choices for your life. In this study, you will find weapons to help you make right choices. One of those is to make the decision right now to like yourself just the way you are. God does. Don't worry about what others think. What do you think about yourself? You were made in the image of God! What an honor that is. God chose you to be alive at this time in history and in this place right now. If God believes you can handle your life here, you can believe it, too.

See yourself the way God sees you. If that means that 100 times a day you have to remind yourself that you are a Mighty Warrior; then do it. The Bible is full of verses that proclaim who you are in Him. Memorize verses like John 3:16 and put your name in place of "the world and whosoever." Study 2 Corinthians 5:17 & 21. Make it personal. Write it down on a paper you put in your wallet; place notes to yourself in your Bible, notebooks, on your computer or cell phone. Constantly remind yourself that you are valuable to God and to every person God has placed around you. You can touch your world (home, school, church, friends, and even enemies) for Christ. You have that much power in you because the Holy Spirit has chosen to live in you. Stand tall and walk in your world as the man of God you were made to be.

Jesus is a great example. He impacted the lives of every person he met and changed the world while a human on Earth. You have that very same power in you. You are a

What If? Freedom Ministries ~ P.O. Box 470252 ~ Tulsa, Oklahoma 74147-0252 ~ 918-249-FREE (3733) ~ www.whatifministires.com

8

Mighty Warrior for God right now. Believe that about yourself. Like yourself. Talk to yourself. (Yes, it is quite healthy to talk to yourself to deposit into your very being what the Word of God says about you.) You are a brave and courageous man. Choose to follow the path God has laid out before you. Being a committed Christian is not for wimps. This is the most courageous decision you may ever make. This choice puts you on the front lines of battle. Be prepared. You are entering a war for your very soul. Knowing and believing who you are in Christ makes you much less vulnerable to the tactics of the devil. Be assured, the enemy does not like men who submit to Christ. However, you are up to the challenge because God is on your side.

You are in this war whether you want to be or not. The question is, "Whose side are you on and how will you fight?" This is not a physical war, but a spiritual one. Understand that you and all youth are a target of the enemy. If Satan can capture the young people, he can win the war. Do not become a prisoner of war. Jesus came to give you freedom and victory over every battle.

This battle for excellence begins in your mind. In our sex-saturated society, you must take the offensive and make a definite choice to think godly thoughts. Remaining pure is not about sex. It is about the mind and heart. Everything you see and hear goes into your mind. In your mind that information becomes thoughts. Those thoughts follow the path to your heart. What you think about becomes a part of who you are. The more you think about something, the more it influences who you become. Jesus said in Matthew 15:18 & 19 (MSG), "What comes out of the mouth gets its start in the heart. It's from the heart that we vomit up evil arguments, murders, adulteries, fornications, thefts, lies, and cussing. That's what pollutes." Think about the influence your family, friends, books, music, the internet, television, and movies have on your mind and heart!

How much TV do you watch? What do you watch? A friend of ours did a simple survey of three major networks in December, 2005, watching each channel for three hours during prime time. Here are some of the results. In just nine hours, there were 124 broken relationships portrayed, 390 incidents of sexually alluring clothing, and 269 sexual innuendoes/behavior. Since that time, programs have only worsened. That does not include commercials. Have you heard the saying, "sex sells"? How can drinking a certain brand of cola make you sexy? It doesn't, but advertisers certainly want you to believe that it does. You are one of the prime targets of their marketing tactics. Do you think they have your best interests at heart? Hardly! It's all about the money. What message do you want to send to the opposite sex? Do you really want to come across as a sex symbol or as a man of God? In light of eternity make the choice to be a man of character. GUARD YOUR HEART AND MIND!

Sexual thoughts are a major part of every man's battle. Left unattended, lustful thoughts can overwhelm you. According to the dictionary, lust is "an overmastering desire; eagerness to possess or enjoy; a desire to gratify the senses; bodily appetite; sexual desire; excessive sexual desire, especially as seeking unrestrained gratification – selfishness." Without restraint, selfish thoughts will destroy you. Yet, our culture seems to put a premium on looking out for number one. If it feels good, do it. We live in an

What If? Freedom Ministries ~ P.O. Box 470252 ~ Tulsa, Oklahoma 74147-0252 ~ 918-249-FREE (3733) ~ www.whatifministires.com

9

instant gratification, all-about-me society. But that is the direct opposite of God's Word. The Bible teaches to give and it will be given to you. If you want to be great, be a servant of mankind. Love your neighbor as yourself. God's Word is meant for your protection, not a means to prevent you from having fun. God made you a sexual being, but He never intended for your thought life to be consumed with sex. When hormones are bouncing and sights and sounds all around you imply that sex is all that matters, it can be difficult to control your thoughts. But you must learn to control them, not give in to them.

To control wrong thinking, it is important to understand the difference between resisting and replacing thoughts. A common mistake we make when attempting to change our thought processes is simply to try to stop thinking about the wrong behavior or bad ideas. This exercise only serves to deepen the activity in your mind, much to the delight of Satan. For example, right now try not to think about a polar bear holding a frosty bottle of Coke in its paw sitting on an iceberg in the middle of the room. Close your eyes; open your eyes; but do not think about the polar bear. Resist those mental images of that polar bear. What happens? The more you try not to think about the polar bear, the more you cannot remove that image from your brain. That is because you are focusing on the thought by trying not to think about it. The more you resist the thought, the more you are drawn to it and the harder it is to get rid of that polar bear. James 4:7 (AMP) can help us understand this. "So be subject to God. Resist the devil (stand firm against him), and he will flee from you." We are instructed to resist the devil, not the thought.

Instead of resisting thoughts, replace them with different and better thoughts. Instead of resisting the polar bear thought, visualize your dream car, favorite football team, or a majestic mountain. Focus on the details of that, and the polar bear disappears. The same is true with impure thoughts. Replace them with honorable ideas. Scripture memorization is extremely important to accomplish this. You need to substitute your warped thoughts with the Truth from The Bible. Memorize helpful verses as part of your ammo for battle. Of course, the devil wants you to believe you cannot memorize scripture. He knows what an effective weapon scripture is against him and your fleshly nature. Do not fall for Satan's tricks. Whom will you believe – Satan, the father of lies, or God? You can do all things through Christ – even memorize Bible verses. An easy way to remember scriptures is to copy them onto 3x5 cards and use them to prompt you to learn each verse you need in your arsenal. Be determined. The excuses can go on forever, or you can decide to hide God's Word in your heart. The more you keep God's Word in your heart and mind, the more you squeeze out the old, stinking thinking.

Imagine your brain as a super computer, the command center for this war. You put data in to get data out; output is determined by the quality of input. Translate this to your mind. If you watch ungodly movies and television programs, think about girls as sex objects, listen to music with violent and disrespectful lyrics, and surf the internet for sexually provocative websites (input), your words and actions (output) will not reflect that of a godly warrior. You are weakening the soldier in you by feeding your thoughts with junk food. On the other hand, if you surround yourself with godly friends, watch, read, and listen to edifying programs, books, and music; study The Bible and seek God's

What If? Freedom Ministries ~ P.O. Box 470252 ~ Tulsa, Oklahoma 74147-0252 ~ 918-249-FREE (3733) ~ www.whatifministires.com

10

will for your life, you are strengthening the warrior within you. Guarding your mind must become a daily discipline to recognize attacks by the enemy.

Back to the computer. Assume you have input all your data and the reports you produced are excellent. Life is great; you feel good about yourself; and praise comes easily. Then you discover your computer has a virus. Oh no! Immediately, you rush to rid the computer of the virus and set up the best detection tools so it will not happen again. Saving your files and adding safeguards become your highest priority. Protecting your mind is so much more important than guarding a computer. How often do you recognize that your mind has a "virus"? Is protecting and renewing your mind your highest priority? What steps do you take to prevent future infestations? How often do you make a reconnaissance of the enemy's camp? Do you have a good battle plan or do you just react to the situation? Your response to protect your mind should be every bit as swift and thorough as your plan to save your computer files. It would be helpful to have a memo that would flash "virus alert" in your mind like the anti-virus software does on your computer. In a way, you do. If you listen, the Holy Spirit flashes warnings in your mind. That uneasiness you feel while leering at a girl is your Holy Spirit virus alert. Oh, that you would shut down your computer (your mind) and reboot through prayer and meditation on God's Word. Be aware; the devil is subtle and a clever liar. Become more sensitive to the Holy Spirit, and take action at the first sign of the enemy infecting your mind.

Look up the following scriptures and write what God speaks to you.

Job 23:10

_____

_____

Proverbs 23:6-7

_____

_____

Jeremiah 1:5

_____

_____

What If? Freedom Ministries ~ P.O. Box 470252 ~ Tulsa, Oklahoma 74147-0252 ~ 918-249-FREE (3733) ~ www.whatifministires.com

11

Jeremiah 29:11

_____

_____

Matthew 5:27-28

_____

_____

2 Corinthians 12:9-10

_____

_____

Memory Verse – Philippians 4:8 (NIV)

Whatever is noble, whatever is right, whatever is pure, whatever is lovely, whatever is admirable – if anything is excellent or praiseworthy – think about such things.

Thinking Points

Write at least five words or phrases that describe the way you see God.

_____

_____

_____

What If? Freedom Ministries ~ P.O. Box 470252 ~ Tulsa, Oklahoma 74147-0252 ~ 918-249-FREE (3733) ~ www.whatifministires.com

12

Describe how you see yourself. Add two things you like about you and two you want to improve.

_____

_____

_____

_____

_____

Which friends and activities have the most positive effect on you? What makes them a positive effect?

_____

_____

_____

Who or what has the most negative effect on you? What makes them a negative effect?

_____

_____

_____

Where do you struggle most in your thought life?

_____

_____

_____

What If? Freedom Ministries ~ P.O. Box 470252 ~ Tulsa, Oklahoma 74147-0252 ~ 918-249-FREE (3733) ~ www.whatifministires.com

13

Write an example that you can use to help you replace a dangerous thought.

_____

_____

_____

Write two or three action points to work on this week to help improve your thinking about God and/or yourself.

_____

_____

_____

What If?
You can never do anything to make God love you any less or any more than He does right now.

What If? Freedom Ministries ~ P.O. Box 470252 ~ Tulsa, Oklahoma 74147-0252 ~ 918-249-FREE (3733) ~ www.whatifministires.com

14

CHAPTER 2
United Front

God created you to be in relationship with Him and others. You were never intended to fight your battles alone. You need people to support and reinforce you. On the battlefield your relationships with fellow warriors are critical. You follow the direction of your Commander with instant and complete obedience along with intense loyalty – even to death. You train together with the soldiers in your unit so that you work and fight as one body. Each person is an integral part of the mission and crucial to each soldier's survival. You must be able trust them with your life. In the military this is accomplished through months of training, living together, and experiencing situations that require total trust of and dependence on the team. Training is so rigid that the unit functions as one by the time they are ready for battle. So too, you must train and build relationships in your life to face the battles not only of your teen years but also in adulthood. The bottom line for winning your war of integrity comes down to relationships with God, others, and yourself.

Where are you in your relationship with God, first and foremost? The biggest step is the wanting to live a righteous life before God and then deciding to do it, enlisting in God's army. Developing character is a process that will take your entire lifetime to achieve. But each day you are obedient to God, the journey is easier. Where is your focus? Is it all about you or about God and others? Sexual temptations like pornography and pre-marital sex are traps set by the enemy to trip you up. Satan would have you believe that God wants to make you miserable and keep you from having fun. That is a lie he used to trick Adam and Eve in the Garden of Eden. In Genesis 3:1 (AMP) it states that, "the serpent was more subtle and crafty than any living creature…" In other words, Satan is a sneaky, devious snake. In verse five, he confused Adam and Eve in the perfect garden by insinuating God was holding out on them, "For God knows that in the day you eat of it your eyes will be opened, and you will be like God, knowing good and evil." The devil still uses deception to persuade unsuspecting soldiers that God is not Who He says He is. Be assured, God withholds no good thing from His children. It is never too late or too early to choose to obey your Commander-in-Chief, Jesus. He loves you more than you can imagine and is waiting to march alongside you on this journey. He is ready to point out the schemes and ambushes planned by the enemy. He will protect you from attacks meant to destroy you. Satan is a formidable foe. **But God** is far above any plot, any weapon, and any tactic the enemy can throw at you. Your secret weapon is that God is on your side; and He knows the enemy's strategy, goes with you into battle, and is all powerful. Trust your Father God.

Every army has training manuals and drill sergeants to prepare new recruits. Your training manual is The Bible, and the Holy Spirit Himself is your drill sergeant. The Bible is full of guidance and strategies to teach you how to win each battle. Think of studying The Word as War College, a time to learn the specifics for daily drills, maneuvers, and strategies. Your Commander inspired the words of The Bible for your safety and protection. If you are afraid, discouraged, confused, or tempted, scripture has

What If? Freedom Ministries ~ P.O. Box 470252 ~ Tulsa, Oklahoma 74147-0252 ~ 918-249-FREE (3733) ~ www.whatifministires.com

15

the answer. If you need direction, comfort, or wisdom, turn to your Bible. God speaks to His men through scripture. Become a student of His Word to know Him better and to understand His ways. Check out these verses to get you started.

Fear – Joshua 1:9

_____

_____

Discouragement – 1 Samuel 30:6

_____

_____

Confusion – 1 Timothy 1:7

_____

_____

Temptation – 1 Corinthians 10:13

_____

_____

Direction – Proverbs 3:5-6

_____

_____

Comfort – 1 Thessalonians 5:9-11

_____

_____

Wisdom – James 1:5

_____

_____

The Creator of the universe wants an intimate relationship with you. He not only created you in His image but also sacrificed His only Son, Jesus, to restore you to fellowship with Him. He loves you – just the way you are. You do not have to clean up your act or make yourself acceptable to have a relationship with Him. In fact, that is counter-productive. He loves you, period. He is your greatest ally and comrade on the battlefield.

What If? Freedom Ministries ~ P.O. Box 470252 ~ Tulsa, Oklahoma 74147-0252 ~ 918-249-FREE (3733) ~ www.whatifministires.com

16

In addition to The Bible, He communicates with you through prayer. Prayer is an essential part of the Christian life. However, it should not feel like an obligation or duty. Although a disciplined, consistent prayer life is important, many Christians turn prayer into a job that requires punching a time clock. Try to think of prayer as a time to spill your guts to God, the good and the bad. But remember, it is two-way communication – listening to Him as well as talking to Him. He inhabits your praises and loves to spend time with you. God is always available. Praying throughout the day is an excellent habit to develop. You don't have to be fancy or pray in "King James" language. Just talk to Him as a Friend. God hears and answers prayer. Jeremiah 33:3 (AMP) confirms His desire, "Call to Me, and I will answer you and show you great and mighty things, which you do not know." He never places you on hold or directs you to voice mail. God wants prayer to become a part of who you are, a part of your very nature. Speak from your heart. Think about this! You, a mere human, have been given the great honor to talk to God, personally, whenever you want. You, a dutiful soldier of God, have that kind of access to your Commander-in-Chief.

Secondly, build relationships with people – family, godly adults, and other teens. Christianity is based on relationships – vertically with God the Father, Son, and Holy Spirit and horizontally with people. Unfortunately, not all teens have a close relationship with their parents or any adult. If that is your case, God will be your Father; but you also need to search for a male role model. In the military there is a chain of command so that every soldier has a more experienced, mature person above him. A raw recruit will not be placed in a position of authority; he must be tested during training and in the heat of battle to be promoted to lead others. The adults God has placed in your life have a wealth of knowledge to help you avoid the pitfalls of war. Learn to value and use the wisdom of those who have walked before you. Try not to focus on the differences and disagreements with your parents or those in authority. Rather, fix your attention on points of agreement, even if they are few. Talk with your parents and godly adults. They are on your side. No matter how difficult this may seem, try it. Begin a little at a time but discuss more than the weather. It may be awkward at first, but understand that your parents want to be a part of your life. Here's a little secret. They are more nervous about talking to you than you are, in most cases. Be the bigger man. You take the initiative and ask to talk often.

Every relationship takes time and effort. Deliberately choose to spend time with your family. You might be surprised how much fun you can have with your entire family if you give them the chance. Playing board games, going fishing or camping, or having a barbeque together are all ways to get to know each other better in non-threatening situations. Spending time with family is also a great way to get to know someone of the opposite sex in a safe environment. (Your parents' goal in life is not to embarrass you. They do want to protect you from harm. Remember, many years ago they were teens too.) Consider establishing regular meetings with your family, both with individuals and groups. You can go out for a soda or coffee, play a game of golf or basketball, or simply schedule dedicated time at home to talk. It's important to keep that time sacred, only for family. Don't blow it off when something else comes up. The time you take to develop

What If? Freedom Ministries ~ P.O. Box 470252 ~ Tulsa, Oklahoma 74147-0252 ~ 918-249-FREE (3733) ~ www.whatifministires.com

17

these relationships will be well worth the effort. Your family can be your greatest ally if you allow them to join your battle.

In addition to family, other godly adults and teens can add an amazing dimension to your life. You cannot fight the battle alone. During wars, soldiers often sacrifice their lives to save a buddy on the battlefield. The intimate relationship developed during training carries over powerfully when engaged with the enemy. Without spending a great amount of time together, that life-giving relationship would be nonexistent. Sadly, visiting face-to-face with even close friends is becoming a lost art in our culture. Between cell phones, text messaging, e-mails, tablets, and so many other technological advances, actually spending time with real people can be a challenge. You can take control of this part of your life and not allow technology to replace personal contact. Rather than text messaging your neighbor, go knock on his door and sit down to talk. Instead of sending e-mails or PMs back and forth, hang out together with your friends. In addition, having earphones plugged in many hours of the day prevents conversation even when you are with people.

Again, relationships take time and effort. Just as you need to work at family relationships, you must make every effort to develop meaningful friendships. You may have many acquaintances, but most people usually have only a few good friends. Time together is a critical element in maintaining good relationships. They do not happen by accident but by your conscious efforts. A good, trustworthy friend is a rare treasure. What kind of friend are you? To have friends you must be a friend. It is a two-way street. If you are a friend who will keep a confidence and be there when needed, you will be rewarded with the same kind of friend.

Consider including a trusted, godly man in your circle of influence. Having friends your own age is important; but knowing an older, wiser man is equally necessary to be a well-rounded and healthy teenager. He might become your mentor or simply be someone you can bounce ideas off when you need to make important decisions. Pray and ask God to show you His choice for you. Select someone that reflects God's love and wisdom and who models what type of man you desire to become. This could be someone you do not know well yet. God enjoys taking you out of your comfort zone to sharpen you into the warrior He wants you to be. Soldiers must conquer their fear of the unknown to go confidently into battle.

Choose your friends wisely. Your peers can be your greatest asset or your worst liability. When you go to war, your life depends on your buddies that surround you. You want disciplined, highly trained soldiers with you when you enter the enemy's territory. You are in a war right where you are. You are in Satan's territory, and you must unite with those who are prepared to fight the battle with you. Good friends will lift you up and point you toward Christ and His goals for your life. They will not ridicule you for taking a stand for doing the right thing but will encourage you to fight with all your might to win your battles.

What If? Freedom Ministries ~ P.O. Box 470252 ~ Tulsa, Oklahoma 74147-0252 ~ 918-249-FREE (3733) ~ www.whatifministires.com

18

On the other hand, wrong influences can pull you away from God and place you in harm's way before you realize what is happening. Do not be deceived. You will become like those with whom you associate. You may believe that you would never lower your standards. Given enough time in the wrong environment, you will make adjustments, little by little, and succumb to the enemy's subtle tactics. He may convince you that you can change the negative influences for the better by spending time with them. That is a noble thought but unlikely to be the case. You will be the one to spiral downward if you continue to surround yourself with ungodly people. When you infiltrate the enemy's camp, be careful that you are not infected with evil. This is not an excuse to avoid caring for others and sharing the gospel. Be a witness of godliness to all those around you, friend or foe. However, your close friends, those with whom you spend time and seek counsel, must be soldiers fighting on your side and not spies in your camp. Your choice of friends determines if your buddies are the kind who will sacrifice their pleasures to help you or sacrifice you to advance their pursuit of pleasure.

As important as it is to have family and godly friends surrounding you, one other relationship is critical to your winning this war. You. The third leg of your strategy is to develop a good relationship with yourself. (Review chapter one if you need to reinforce how you think about yourself.) Statistics show that many teens do not like themselves. You may feel you have failed so many times that you are hopeless. But you know, without Jesus, everyone is hopeless. That can be a good place because it forces you to look at God as your only source of help. He made you to be a warrior. From creation, God intended the man to be the provider and protector of the human race. He has given you the ability and the weapons to succeed at this task. With that knowledge, you can be a confident soldier as you enter each battle. Train your mind to believe what God's Word says about you. You are amazing because He made you just the way you are. You are not a mistake. You are so awesome in God's eyes. Don't sell yourself short. You are not a piece of junk but God's trophy. When you see yourself through God's eyes, it becomes easier to say "no" to the temptations of this world.

Spend some time studying the following scriptures and write God's insight to you in the spaces provided.

Psalm 40:1-2

_____

_____

What If? Freedom Ministries ~ P.O. Box 470252 ~ Tulsa, Oklahoma 74147-0252 ~ 918-249-FREE (3733) ~ www.whatifministires.com

19

Proverbs 8:17

_____

_____

Proverbs 13:20

_____

_____

Mark 7:10

_____

_____

John 15:15-17

_____

_____

Romans 8:37-39

_____

_____

2 Corinthians 6:18

_____

_____

What If? Freedom Ministries ~ P.O. Box 470252 ~ Tulsa, Oklahoma 74147-0252 ~ 918-249-FREE (3733) ~ www.whatifministires.com

20

Ephesians 1:3-6

_____

_____

Memory Verse – Psalm 27:4 (NIV)

One thing I ask of the Lord, this is what I seek: that I may dwell in the house of the Lord all the days of my life, to gaze upon the beauty of the Lord, and to seek Him in His temple.

Thinking Points

Circle the option that best describes the following:

A. Your relationship with God right now

Excellent   Good   Neither Good or Bad   Fair   Poor

B. Your relationship with your parents/adult authority figure

Excellent   Good   Neither Good or Bad   Fair   Poor

C. Your relationship with other teens

Excellent   Good   Neither Good or Bad   Fair   Poor

D. Your relationship with yourself

Excellent   Good   Neither Good or Bad   Fair   Poor

What If? Freedom Ministries ~ P.O. Box 470252 ~ Tulsa, Oklahoma 74147-0252 ~ 918-249-FREE (3733) ~ www.whatifministires.com

21

Write one thing that you can do to improve each of the following relationships.

God

_____

_____

Parents/adult authority figure

_____

_____

Teens/Peers/Friends

_____

_____

Write three things you like about yourself.

_____

_____

List one good thing about each relationship.

God

_____

_____

Parents/adult authority figure

_____

_____

What If? Freedom Ministries ~ P.O. Box 470252 ~ Tulsa, Oklahoma 74147-0252 ~ 918-249-FREE (3733) ~ www.whatifministires.com

22

Teens/Peers/Friends

_____

_____

Write three things you like about yourself.

_____

_____

_____

What is the one thing you would most like to improve about yourself? What is your first step?

_____

_____

_____

Write one action point regarding relationships that you will work on this week.

_____

_____

_____

What If?
God really wants to be your closest Friend and spend time with you every day.

What If? Freedom Ministries ~ P.O. Box 470252 ~ Tulsa, Oklahoma 74147-0252 ~ 918-249-FREE (3733) ~ www.whatifministires.com

23

What If? Freedom Ministries ~ P.O. Box 470252 ~ Tulsa, Oklahoma 74147-0252 ~ 918-249-FREE (3733) ~ www.whatifministires.com

24

CHAPTER 3
The Environment of War

In military boot camp and training exercises, the soldiers' environment is limited to only those activities that support the goal of the training – to win on the battlefield. Anything that will distract the soldiers from focusing on their mission must be eliminated. They may be isolated from others or forced to live 24/7 with their unit. What they eat, where and how much they sleep, how they travel, what they think about – everything they do is controlled by the commanders as a means to achieve the desired goal. That goal is to be prepared for the assigned mission plus any possible ambush from the enemy. Their lives depend on how well they have integrated the lessons so that in the heat of battle nothing can distract them. The soldiers enter battle so focused on the objective that they perform their responsibilities instinctively. The intense preparation creates warriors ready to enter battle with confidence. Their minds and bodies react automatically according to their training. They may feel fear, but they act with courage in the face of the enemy because they are totally focused on the mission – to win. Where is your focus? Are you willing to lay aside your diversions to be able to win your war?

You are in this battle called life whether you like it or not. Your preparation during childhood and now as a teen determines how effectively you can fight the enemy. That training is every bit as important as the military maneuvers practiced in boot camp. However, most of you do not have the discipline of the drill sergeant forced upon you. You are basically free to choose what you do, wear, eat, listen to, and watch. Along with that freedom comes great responsibility. Either you control your environment or you allow others to control it. Think about these examples.

- If someone says "Rocky Balboa," you probably see Sylvester Stallone running up those steps in Philadelphia and hear the movie's theme song in your mind. You may even start shadow boxing to mimic Rocky.
- What happens if you are raiding the refrigerator and suddenly hear the music that introduces Monday night football? What images come to mind? You may turn around and tackle your buddy reaching for a slice of pizza.
- If you are stopped at a traffic light and the truck of your dreams pulls up next to you, do you ignore it or visualize yourself behind the wheel?

In each instance, a particular stimulus controlled your environment. No one had to tell you how to respond to those images or sounds; each reaction was automatic.

What you see, hear, taste, touch and smell affects your body by stimulating the brain. The three previous examples controlled your environment, if only briefly, and thus your responses. Your environment – all the conditions, circumstances, and influences surrounding you – plays a critical role in your battle plan. Obviously, you cannot control everything in your life. You did not choose your family, where you live, or your family's income level. You cannot change those things, so you must learn to live with them. It is your choice whether you love and honor your parents. You decide how you will treat

What If? Freedom Ministries ~ P.O. Box 470252 ~ Tulsa, Oklahoma 74147-0252 ~ 918-249-FREE (3733) ~ www.whatifministires.com

25

your brothers and sisters. You can be thankful you have a home and food on the table, or you can complain about the circumstances of your life. It is up to you. **You cannot control the circumstances, but you CAN control your attitude toward them.**

Think about the things you can control. Do you complete your homework diligently or half-heartedly? Do you read books and magazines that build you up or focus on gratifying your flesh? What kind of music do you listen to? What movies and TV programs do you watch? What do you do for fun? Who is in your circle of influence? You have much more control over your life than you may realize. Strategic choices are made on the battlefield every day. Each decision determines the direction of your battle. Are you more influenced by good or evil? The devil wants to be in command of your environment and will use any trick he can to do so. You must take charge of your surroundings if you are to win the battle for integrity.

Everywhere you turn, you have opportunities to make choices, right or wrong, regarding your sexuality. Avoiding sexual temptation is a full-time job. Pornography, anything that causes you to lust after the flesh, is a mighty weapon of Satan. He understands how you are made and what impulses lie within you. And he is a master of deception. He instigated the "if it feels good, do it" culture. He wants you to focus on the moment, not on possible consequences of poor choices. Given the opportunity, he will persuade you that his way is more fun and rewarding than God's way. He still uses the words, "Surely, God has not said …." His strategy is to convince you that what God made for good should be used for evil. God created sex and the hormones that are raging in your body. He designed your body to work the way it does. He is not surprised that you struggle with impure sexual thoughts. However, **you do not** have to give into the temptations of your thoughts. Having bad thoughts is not sin. Acting on wrong thoughts is. You can control your environment to minimize exposure to the temptations, the enemy's ambushes and plots. You can change the channel, walk away, close the cover, refuse to participate. The choice is yours.

One of Satan's favorite playgrounds is in the area of sexuality. What is the man's primary sex organ? No. It's a few feet above that. A man's primary sex organ is the brain. A woman's is the heart. Women are relational and stimulated emotionally. As a man, you are predominantly stimulated sexually by visual cues. So what you view with your eyes triggers certain sensations in your brain automatically. God created you that way.

Your brain is an amazing organ with remarkable abilities. Remember the images of "Rocky," Monday night football, and the dream truck? Each one of those created a response in you. Did you have to think about your response? No. Those were all automatic responses triggered by the environment those words generated. Likewise, do you have to remind yourself to breathe or tell your heart to beat? Your heart beats, the digestive system secretes enzymes, and the lungs breathe whether you remind them to or not. If you had to manage those functions on a day-to-day basis, you would die. That's why God built the autonomic nervous system in you.

What If? Freedom Ministries ~ P.O. Box 470252 ~ Tulsa, Oklahoma 74147-0252 ~ 918-249-FREE (3733) ~ www.whatifministires.com

26

What you allow into your environment can also trigger automatic responses. When you see a girl with a great body (environment), you can stare and allow inappropriate images to flood your brain or you can divert your eyes. If you watch a movie that is filled with racy love scenes, your environment is reinforcing negative sexual behavior and providing opportunities for even the strongest warrior to sin. When you view pornography, your heart pounds, your palms sweat, breathing increases, body temperature rises, other secretions constrict certain blood vessels, and suddenly, automatically, you have an erection. God created those hormones and designed your body to work the way it does. But, He intended those sexual arousals for marriage. Even though they come alive during the teen years, you can put those urges to sleep until you are ready for marriage by controlling your environment. Who controls your environment? **YOU DO!** What you listen to and what you see affects your brain. Your tactic must be to learn to avoid ungodly opportunities that can create a negative autonomic response and to control the automatic responses of the body with your mind and the help of God.

In war, the one who controls the environment will win the battle.

Here are some tips to help you control your environment. These and others will be discussed in detail in a later lesson.

- Be aware of what triggers automatic, negative responses so you can avoid them. Triggers are anything that causes you to think or act in a specific way. A picture, a billboard, provocative commercials, or sexually explicit song lyrics are just a few possible triggers. Certain people can also trigger wrong responses in you.

- Choose your friends and those you hang out with wisely. You will become like them – for better or worse.

- Set boundaries. Like soldiers establish their encampment and perimeter, you can set boundaries around your environment to establish your personal perimeter. Determine what those boundaries are, and stick to them. Don't allow yourself to get into situations that make it easy for you to violate your boundaries.

- Learn to bounce your eyes. If you see a girl dressed provocatively, don't leer. Bounce your eyes and thoughts to something else. If you drive past a billboard that uses sex to sell, look away immediately.

- Be careful in selecting the movies you watch. If you realize you made a mistake in the choice of a movie, walk out. Do not allow yourself to be sabotaged by inaction or the fear of embarrassment.

- Turn off the television, radio, or computer. If you have trouble resisting any of these, **TURN THEM OFF!**

  o Carefully select what TV programs you watch to minimize the chances of sinning with your eyes. Remember, men are visually stimulated.

What If? Freedom Ministries ~ P.O. Box 470252 ~ Tulsa, Oklahoma 74147-0252 ~ 918-249-FREE (3733) ~ www.whatifministires.com

27

- Know what types of music radio stations play, and listen only to those stations that play uplifting songs.
- Do not go online without a good filter to prevent pornography from appearing on your screen.

Consider the story of Abraham and Lot. Read it in Genesis 13:5-13 and 19:1-17. Abraham, one of Christianity's pillars of faith, was a righteous man. He trusted God enough to leave his home and family and to move his entire household to an unknown destination. Lot, his nephew, traveled with him and spent many years under the leadership of Abraham who taught him the ways of God. Lot enjoyed all the advantages of living with the patriarch of the Jewish nation. His environment was excellent. Over time, Abraham's and Lot's herds and flocks increased greatly. Since their herdsmen began bickering over the availability of water and pasture, the men separated to avoid discord between the two families. Abraham trusted God enough to give Lot first pick of where he would live. Lot decided to move to Sodom – a very bad decision. He surrounded himself with evil. Genesis 13:13 (NIV) states, "Now the men of Sodom were wicked and were sinning greatly against the Lord." Lot deliberately placed himself in a bad environment despite his godly upbringing. He considered the prosperous, physical features of the land but placed little importance on the spiritual consequences. He never dreamed that he would lower his standards to the point of putting his whole family in jeopardy. In the end, Lot lost his wealth and wife to Sodom and Gomorrah and nearly forfeited his entire family – all because he chose to stay in the wrong place surrounded by the wrong people. Your environment holds a powerful influence over you. Learn a lesson from Lot.

Only you can protect your environment. This requires constant vigilance on your part. The enemy is subtle and has practiced his warfare tactics throughout history. You are part of this war. Are you in the war to win or to give in to the adversary? You cannot compromise and participate in the war half-heartedly. Either you fight your enemy or you will be defeated. Protect your borders and guard your heart.

Use the provided space to write your thoughts about the following scriptures.

Job 31:1-2

_____

_____

What If? Freedom Ministries ~ P.O. Box 470252 ~ Tulsa, Oklahoma 74147-0252 ~ 918-249-FREE (3733) ~ www.whatifministires.com

28

Matthew 5:28

_____

_____

1 Corinthians 15:33

_____

_____

2 Corinthians 6:14-16

_____

_____

Galatians 5:16-17

_____

_____

If you want to study more about the environment of war, read Romans 8, especially verses 1-18. It discusses the pros and cons of the environments of the secular and the spirit worlds. Think about how you are living your life compared to what these scriptures teach.

_____

_____

_____

_____

_____

What If? Freedom Ministries ~ P.O. Box 470252 ~ Tulsa, Oklahoma 74147-0252 ~ 918-249-FREE (3733) ~ www.whatifministires.com

29

Memory verse – 1 Corinthians 10:13 (NIV)

No temptation has seized you except what is common to man. And God is faithful; he will not let you be tempted beyond what you can bear. But when you are tempted, he will also provide a way out so that you can stand up under it.

Thinking Points

What are some of the diversions in your environment? What can you do to minimize them?

_____

_____

_____

Give an example of how you can control your attitude in the midst of a bad circumstance.

_____

_____

_____

How do you allow others to control your environment? What can you do to improve this?

_____

_____

_____

What are some ways you can minimize your exposure to an ambush of the devil?

_____

_____

_____

What If? Freedom Ministries ~ P.O. Box 470252 ~ Tulsa, Oklahoma 74147-0252 ~ 918-249-FREE (3733) ~ www.whatifministires.com

30

Write one strategy you will put into practice this week to improve your environment.

_____

_____

_____

What If?
God planned for you to live right where you are, in this time in history, and with the people and circumstances around you just so you could impact your environment in a powerful way.

What If? Freedom Ministries ~ P.O. Box 470252 ~ Tulsa, Oklahoma 74147-0252 ~ 918-249-FREE (3733) ~ www.whatifministires.com

31

What If? Freedom Ministries ~ P.O. Box 470252 ~ Tulsa, Oklahoma 74147-0252 ~ 918-249-FREE (3733) ~ www.whatifministires.com

32

CHAPTER 4
Cyber Warfare

The war for your life is more intense than at any other time in history. Satan is fighting hard to win over the minds of young people. Consider a lesson from history. In the 1930's, one of the most effective tools that Adolph Hitler used to infect the German people with his ideology was the Hitler Youth Movement. Children were recruited and taught his Nazi propaganda at schools, clubs, sports – everywhere. The rewards and prestige that went along with belonging to his group were great. In a very short time the children of Germany were so indoctrinated with Hitler's lies that they turned on their parents, other family members, and anyone who even hinted of not supporting Nazism. In a few years, they were old enough to enter the physical battle and ready to follow Hitler blindly. Hitler's Youth tortured, maimed, betrayed, and murdered millions.

The technology age has made it easier than ever before to attack teens with weapons that are amazingly powerful when it comes to trapping your mind and body. You are bombarded from all directions with temptations that are designed to weaken and destroy you. Sexual messages are everywhere. You can lower your standards without realizing it when inappropriate images are commonplace. It is difficult to keep your mind and eyes from sinning in normal, every day life. Add to that, you are the target of the pornography industry. You can easily feel overwhelmed by the enemy and believe that the war is impossible to win. That is exactly what the devil wants you to think. Deception is a strong weapon in any war, especially the war for your mind. Remember, the battlefield is your mind. Truth is one of your greatest weapons. Satan is threatened by sexual truth (mentally and physically), and he will do anything he can to lead you down the wrong path. Don't listen to his lies. Arm yourself with Truth.

Before you go any further, please read Phil's story about his 40-year struggle with pornography addiction. It is an ugly, but true story that has a very happy ending. Praise God!

PHIL'S STORY

As a young boy, I was exposed to pornography through magazines in my home. I was hooked almost immediately. I read all the articles and memorized the pictures. Those images haunted me for 40 years while pornography ruled my life. During my teens, I was depressed and avoided relationships. I was not a good student or popular at school, so I used sports to help me cope with the loneliness and misery. I looked at girls with one thought in mind. And it was not a pure thought. Females were objects to be used for my pleasure and deserved no respect. I was filled with hate and anger. I hated myself because of my secret addiction and expressed that hatred toward others around me. Respect was a foreign idea. I was consumed with the selfishness of pornography. Everything was ALL ABOUT ME! My life was miserable.

From early childhood, pornography addiction ruled my life just like drugs control the life of a drug addict. I always had to have more; my lust was never satisfied. Because of the

What If? Freedom Ministries ~ P.O. Box 470252 ~ Tulsa, Oklahoma 74147-0252 ~ 918-249-FREE (3733) ~ www.whatifministires.com

33

fantasy world I lived in, my life spiraled out of control. School was drudgery, my job performance suffered; I had no real friends; I created fear and dysfunction in my family; and my marriage nearly ended in divorce. I was miserable and used the fantasy life of pornography to convince myself that everything was just the way I wanted it to be. Everyone around me was the problem, not me. The women in my fantasies never disagreed with me; their role in my mind was to give me pleasure – whatever that was at the moment. I retreated into my world of pornography to avoid the reality of the mess I had made of my life.

I had to wear masks to protect my secret life. The public masks portrayed the loving husband, caring father, devout church member, and professional Air Force pilot. But in private the masks came off and revealed an explosive, sarcastic, bitter, angry man. No one knew the real me; I wouldn't let them. That was too dangerous. They might find out who I really was, so I had no true friends. This was my life as a porn addict for over 40 years. When given the choice between pornography and my family, pornography won. I separated from my wife of twenty-six years. During our seven-year separation, I tried to fix myself hundreds of times – without success. In the fall of 2001, I began a Christian 12-step recovery program called Celebrate Recovery. (They have groups for teens, too.) Only after I totally surrendered to Jesus Christ was I able to experience true freedom and happiness. The program was one of the hardest things I have ever done. It was painful looking at my life honestly and accepting responsibility for my behavior and wrong choices. But it was also one of the best things I have ever accomplished. My life has changed dramatically. I am a new man with freedom in Christ. Please, listen to my warning about the dangers of pornography and give the Freedom of Christ a chance.

If someone would have told me as a teenager that pornography would control my life for the next forty years, I would have called him a liar. **I** was in control. **I** knew my limits. **I** was invincible – I thought. Not until I gave up control of my life did I realize that God had created my sexual desires for my bride Even though I violated the marriage bed by viewing pornography, God never gave up on me. I had lost a treasure in my beloved wife because of my selfish desires. But God forgave me; Bobi has forgiven me; my children forgave me; and I have forgiven myself. I am restored. That is the good news of my story. No matter how bad I was, no matter how long I wallowed in the pit of pornography, **God never gave up on me! God** loved me when I could not love myself. **God** loved me when I hated Him. **God** cares about you that very same way. There is nothing you have done or ever will do that will change God's loving attitude toward you. That's it, pure and simple. He is wanting, willing, and waiting to restore you. God is the God of restoration.

BOBI'S STORY

Throughout my school years, I struggled with low self-esteem and fear. Even though I grew up in the church, I did not feel loved and ached for attention. A big people pleaser, I tried to do anything to get people to like me. But my efforts were never enough. I really did love God but struggled with a religion of "don'ts" and an abusive atmosphere in our home. To overcome my low self-esteem, I buried myself in my schoolwork and

What If? Freedom Ministries ~ P.O. Box 470252 ~ Tulsa, Oklahoma 74147-0252 ~ 918-249-FREE (3733) ~ www.whatifministires.com

34

extra-curricular activities. I belonged to many clubs and competed on the gymnastics team. I received most of my positive attention from my teachers and through school activities. I was not popular in school. I participated in many activities but was never one of "the group." I used busy-ness to try to fill the voids in my life. But, that was never enough. I needed relationships. There were some, but loneliness and insecurity were always with me.

When I left home for college, I thought getting away from my family and circumstances would make me happy. It didn't. I still had to live with myself. And I did not like me. I was a control freak, a manipulator, and a very co-dependent young woman. I had a dream that if only I could find a man to love me and take care of me, my world would be complete. I married Phil with that vision in mind. Our marriage was anything but a fairytale. We both came to our marriage with our own individual problems. We eventually learned that two emotionally unhealthy people cannot make a healthy marriage. When I reached my lowest point, I was miserable, depressed, and suicidal. That is the place where I asked God to do whatever it took to change me into the woman He wanted me to be. It was a long process, but God was faithful to complete an amazing work in my life.

One of the first things I had to do was to learn to like myself and see me through God's eyes. He loved me just the way I was. That was an incredible revelation to me since I had never seemed to be loved for who I was but only for what I did. Over several years as I studied The Bible and learned from some excellent teachers and mentors, I changed. My circumstances did not change at first. Even though I had no idea Phil was addicted to pornography, his addiction affected my life daily. I had to learn to see myself as a woman of God no matter how I was treated. Gradually, God transformed me into a godly woman who is confident in who I am in Christ. It was not an easy process, but the peace and joy I have now make every step worthwhile. To add to that, God also worked a miracle in Phil's life and our marriage. If God can re-create us in His image, He can do anything. He truly took the rags and ugliness of our lives and made something beautiful. We share our story with the hope that we can help you make positive changes and wise choices early in your life.

Our story had a miraculous ending. But it would have been so much better if Phil had never traveled down the path of pornography and sexual addiction. Pornography had a devastating impact on both our lives. That is why we are so passionate about educating you about its dangers. To fight this fight well, you must recognize the weapons of the enemy. What are some examples of pornography? Take some time right now to write down a few before continuing.

_____

_____

So what did you come up with? Do you consider any music videos or sit coms, Victoria Secrets catalogs and fashion shows, or Sports Illustrated Swim Suit Edition to be

What If? Freedom Ministries ~ P.O. Box 470252 ~ Tulsa, Oklahoma 74147-0252 ~ 918-249-FREE (3733) ~ www.whatifministires.com

35

pornography? Yes, all of these and so much more are full of pornographic images. First, what is pornography? It is any material that arouses lustful, sexual desire. That could include photos, videos, nudity, or printed words. Here's another question for you. Remember what your primary sex organ is? The brain, where images are interpreted and sent throughout your body, is your principal sex organ. As a man, you are predominantly stimulated sexually by visual cues. God created you that way. What you view with your eyes triggers certain sensations in your brain automatically. The more you think about those images, the more they stay in your brain.

Muscle memory can help explain how that happens. Phil was a gymnast during his teens and college years. (He was quite good at it, too.) When he wanted to learn a new skill, he had to do strength and conditioning exercises to prepare before he could perform the skill. For example, he had to build muscle mass when he was learning to do the iron cross on still rings. Every day he tried to lower his body a little more to reach the goal of his arms being parallel to the floor while supporting the weight of his entire body. Every day his muscles were learning what to do. He practiced the cross multiple times at every workout to train his muscles. Over many months, his body grew stronger and memorized what the muscles needed to do to attain the cross position. He finally reached the point that he did not have to strain or think about what he had to do for the iron cross. It became an automatic response to perform that skill.

The same process happens when you look at pornography. Popular opinion today says you can look at porn without creating a problem. Every guy does it. Right? **WRONG!** You cannot look at pornography without negative effects. Granted, some can look and walk away. Many cannot walk away. Every time you look, muscle memory goes into action. The grooves in your brain are etched deeper and deeper every time an image appears in the brain. The images can become so deeply embedded that without a miracle from God, you cannot erase them from your mind. Do not take that first step onto the slippery slope.

Have you ever been on a particularly slick, icy hill? You know the ones that when you take one step forward, whoosh, you're at the bottom before you know it – out of control, unable to stop, and knocking over others on the way down the hill. So it is with taking one look at pornography whether it is in a magazine, on the net, or in mom's lingerie catalog. You are taking the risk of ending up at the bottom of the hill involved in things you never imagined or vowed you would never do.

Opportunities to view pornography are everywhere. That is a sad thing in today's society. But what is increasingly disturbing is the attitude of young people toward pornography. When asked about pornography, many teens immediately respond with the word "normal." **PORNOGRAPHY IS NOT NORMAL!** It does not matter how widespread it is in today's culture, it is not normal; and it is definitely not God's best for you. Pornography is degrading, disrespectful, addictive, and dishonoring to God, yourself, and others. It has the power to trivialize crimes like incest, child molestation, and rape. Both teens and adults have been desensitized by various media regarding pornography and sexual purity. **GUARD YOUR EYES AND EARS!**

What If? Freedom Ministries ~ P.O. Box 470252 ~ Tulsa, Oklahoma 74147-0252 ~ 918-249-FREE (3733) ~ www.whatifministires.com

36

This is not easy, but you can do it. You live in a society where girls' clothing styles are designed to reveal way more than you need to see and to tempt you to give in to the deception of the enemy. You are challenged each day with the following and more:

- Short skirts, plunging necklines, tight fitting clothes, see-through outfits and material that clings to every curve – all are promoted as fashionable and stylish.
- TV programs include everything from sex outside of marriage, having sex on the first date, homosexuality, stars dressed in as little clothing as possible – all presented as socially acceptable behavior and something to be copied. It is difficult to find a prime-time program that does not offend Judeo-Christian standards.
- Commercials use sex to sell everything from hamburgers, cars, hair products, and cell phones. What was considered pornography only a few years ago is portrayed as good advertising today.
- In the fall of 2005, the state of Oregon passed a law that legalized live sex acts on stage. In some states pornography appears to be more protected under the law than the rights of Christians.

Over time, standards have been lowered so that you have become desensitized to what is evil in God's eyes. Not that many years ago, a young lady was never seen with a young man without a chaperone; clothing covered most of a woman's body; and "no PDA" meant no public display of affection. In the mid sixties the sexuality of America changed dramatically. "Free love" and "burn the bra" were popular slogans. In only a few years it became fashionable to wear clothing that exposed more curves and flesh that only women of the street would have worn just a few years before. Sleeping together, that is having sexual intercourse, before marriage gained acceptance as the new "freedoms" became more recognized. In less than one generation dress codes were dropped from schools. Respect for the opposite sex and the stigma of losing your virginity before your wedding day have all but disappeared. The culture you live in is determined to destroy young men of character. Your challenge is to fight for your very life.

Satan's approach is to destroy the morals and godliness of young people. It is gradual and calculated. You are now part of a generation that has grown up without the moral restraints that previously protected the youth of America. The downward slide has been executed so cleverly that many still have not realized what has happened. Little by little standards have been lowered. Young people who want to do what is right **seem** to be in the minority. When those around you buy into the marketing schemes that promote scanty clothing, rebellion, and selfishness, it can be difficult to stand firm. That is when you pray, recite memory verses, and ask your support group for help. These tactics anger your adversary. Resist peer pressure and the downward spiral of society with all your strength. Learn a lesson from the frog. If you put a frog in a pan of cold water on the stove and heat the water gradually, the frog will make no effort to escape his death trap. The frog continually adjusts to the temperature of the water until it dies, unaware of the danger all around him. DON'T BE A FROG!

What If? Freedom Ministries ~ P.O. Box 470252 ~ Tulsa, Oklahoma 74147-0252 ~ 918-249-FREE (3733) ~ www.whatifministires.com

37

You must remain watchful in this battle. Just like a lookout in the military, train yourself to watch for the subtle and not-so-subtle attacks against you. Make yourself aware of your environment and steer clear of places that you know will test your limits as a warrior. You may need to avoid certain stores at the mall; particular TV programs, movies, and music; and even some of your friends. Only you can accept the responsibility to make right choices daily to protect yourself from attack. This is no easy task, especially with the advent of the internet. The internet can be used for good or evil. You have access to more information through the internet than ever before in history. That access can open a world of opportunities for you to grow and reach your potential. However, it can have just as powerful an effect for evil. The pornography industry uses the internet masterfully to target you, mighty man of God.

Pornography entices curious minds to take one look at the forbidden. Peer pressure to "be a man" leads many soldiers into the enemy's camp. Beware! Studies have shown that pornography is every bit as addictive as cocaine or heroin. Addictions are progressive. Here is another story of a man, Ken, who fell into the pornography trap. His addiction began when he was eleven years old. Even though he was a Christian, he struggled with his secret fantasies throughout his teen and college years. Upon graduation, he became a school teacher. When he married a beautiful Christian girl, he thought his problem would go away. It did not. The secret merely went deeper. His lies were exposed six years into the marriage when they received a $300.00 phone bill full of calls to porn numbers. His explanation was that he had become bored just looking at pictures and needed more to feed his habit. At his wife's insistence, Ken entered counseling. He went through the motions during his sessions so that he could be finished with it and get back to his fantasy world.

His cravings could not be satisfied, so the phone calls progressed to letter writing asking women to meet him for sex. He visited adult movie houses and acted out hoping that a woman might join him in his activities. Needing a bigger thrill, videos and magazines were replaced by the internet. His life was so out of control that he would begin planning his sexual activities in his mind the minute his wife left for work. His behavior became more erotic and dangerous as bills began adding up and straining the household budget. His marriage was becoming worse every day, and divorce was imminent. He began cruising bad areas of town looking for prostitutes and bigger thrills to feed his addiction. His "problem" was taking on a life of its own. Finally, his habit cost him his job, because he had viewed pornographic websites on his computer at the school where he taught. He knew how risky his behavior was, but the lustful drives of his addiction overruled common sense.

Fortunately, Ken's story has a happy ending. Losing his job was a major wake-up call. God had his attention, and Ken's healing began. Like Phil, Ken joined a Celebrate Recovery group to support him on his road to recovery. He learned that God is a God of recovery and restoration. He now walks daily with his heavenly Father and guards his mind vigilantly. God continues to restore him and his marriage. Now, he is free and asked to add his story of the progression of sexual addiction in this manual to warn young men about the serious dangers of pornography.

What If? Freedom Ministries ~ P.O. Box 470252 ~ Tulsa, Oklahoma 74147-0252 ~ 918-249-FREE (3733) ~ www.whatifministires.com

38

For many, just one visit to a web-site with a sexually enticing image is all it takes to be hooked. Pop ups and deceptive e-mails can trap you before you realize what has happened. Entering an innocent word in a search field that leads to porn sites is a diabolical strategy of the devil. One image can be enough to destroy your resolve and lure you back; you crave more to feed your flesh. But that appetite can never be satisfied. Each time you allow your imagination to slip into pornography, that fantasy world, you deepen that groove in your brain. Surfing the internet unfiltered, watching a sexually enticing advertisement on TV, or viewing an R or X-rated movie reinforces the grooves so that each time it becomes an easier and more automatic response in your mind. Look away immediately; bounce your eyes; and replace the images with The Word of God. You must practice; run training drills daily to make this an automatic response when in the heat of battle. Remember, the enemy will attack you when you least expect it. Be ready before the attack comes. Anticipate situations that trigger wrong responses so that you evade the tricks of your opponent.

Even if you work hard to avoid pornography on the net, you may accidentally find yourself behind enemy lines. Satan knows even one look can weaken a soldier. Porn can quickly take control when you surrender to your fleshly impulses. Even strong, well-disciplined soldiers can fall prey. Have your winning strategy in place. The more weapons in your arsenal and the bigger your army, the safer it is for you.

- Never go to a porn site intentionally.
- Install a good filter on your computer. Never use a computer that does not have a filter.
- Place your computer with the screen facing out in a room used by the entire family. Using a computer in your room provides too many opportunities for secrecy. Darkness and secrecy are the devil's territory. Fight him on your ground, not his.
- If you find yourself in a porn site accidentally, get out immediately. Do not give an opening to your enemy to infiltrate your mind.
- Notify your parents any time inappropriate materials appear on the computer.
- Ask your parents to help you by monitoring your internet use.
- Do not respond to PMs or texting from any unknown parties.

You will not hear discussions on this next topic very often in church groups. But it is one that affects most warriors and needs to be brought out into the open. That word is masturbation. As you go through puberty, your body makes many changes sexually. It is common for young men to experience waking up to find they have an erection or have had a wet dream, an ejaculation while asleep. These are normal phenomena that happen due to hormonal changes in your body. However, masturbation is something different. It is purposely manipulating yourself for sexual pleasure without culminating in sexual intercourse with your wife. Please note the word "wife." God created sex and said it is good. But He intended it to be experienced only in the context of marriage. Then it is very good. With your hormones and society shouting that you need to have sex, that you have a right to experience sex, it is hard to resist. Hard, but not impossible. A good soldier trains himself to withstand interrogations and torture. You must train yourself to

What If? Freedom Ministries ~ P.O. Box 470252 ~ Tulsa, Oklahoma 74147-0252 ~ 918-249-FREE (3733) ~ www.whatifministires.com

39

withstand the torture of sexual temptation. You can do this! You are strong and mighty in God. A good soldier can do whatever he sets his mind to do. Set your mind to remain firm in your resolve to be a man of honor. God never intended masturbation to be used as a substitute for sexual intercourse. This is NOT a tool to use so that you can say you are saving yourself for marriage.

Since viewing pornography affects your mind and leads to sexual arousal, it often ends in masturbation. Self sex completes the cycle of porn. That groove that is etched in your brain every time a pornographic image appears grows much deeper when you masturbate. The heightened emotional response during an orgasm doubly implants the images in the brain. The addictive cycle is reinforced and made stronger each time viewing images coincides with masturbation. This is a dangerous, self-perpetuating mine field. If you are trapped in this prison of the devil, seek help immediately. Your father, pastor, or mentor would be a good starting point. Remember, God gave you the gift of your sexuality to be shared with your wife. Sexual solitaire is not what God had in mind when he created sex. Saving yourself for your wife is an act of obedience that all good warriors must strive to achieve.

Perhaps you have gone beyond masturbation and have experimented sexually. In many circles the stigma of being a virgin is a laughable offense. Pregnancy out of wedlock is commonplace, and having sex is a sign of "manhood." **LIE!** The attitude among young men that casual sex is a game of conquest to be bragged about in the locker room is a sign of weakness. A teen who is not strong enough to resist peer pressure or to control his sexual appetite is not demonstrating strength and maturity. Going along with the crowd and giving in to sexual urges do not prove your manhood. You don't control your sexual appetite, so you take the precious gift of virginity from a girl and her future husband. Do not fall for the tactic that if you "love" her and plan to marry her, it is acceptable to stretch the sexual boundaries even to the point of intercourse. If you truly love her, you will honor and respect her enough to wait for the wedding night. Sexual sin is a wound against her body and your body. A true warrior respects himself and the girl he is with enough to avoid sexual intimacy. Remember, that includes the mind and emotions as well as physical contact.

Understand that girls are emotional beings. Whereas men are visual characters and often think of sex as a one time physical release, girls are relational creatures. When a girl gives in to your advances, she is giving away a part of her heart. The emotional consequences can be enormous. Girls who have sex before marriage tend to suffer from depression, and a great majority of them contemplate or attempt suicide. Do you really want to be a part of that? Do not toy with a girl's heart. Honor her as a person of value, a treasure, created in God's image. So what is a soldier to do? Train your mind ahead of time. Just as physical conditioning and ten-mile marches prepare the troops for long, hard battles, you must perform your own mental calisthenics for combat. Determine in advance that you will not allow yourself to fall into situations that make it easy for your hormones to overtake you. Don't spend time alone with your girlfriend. Each time you are alone your defenses break down a little bit more until eventually the perimeter is compromised and you go down a path you never intended. Exercise. Yes, physical

What If? Freedom Ministries ~ P.O. Box 470252 ~ Tulsa, Oklahoma 74147-0252 ~ 918-249-FREE (3733) ~ www.whatifministires.com

40

activity can release sexual tension. You can learn to control your responses to sexual stimulus through physical exercise. Just as your body has autonomic responses, you can train your mind and body to have positive automatic responses to sexual temptation. The enemy has traps laid out all around you. Be smart. Recognize the pitfalls and avoid them so that the devil cannot tempt you to touch a girl inappropriately.

Another attack against your manhood is aggressive girls. Until recently, young men pursued the female. Nowadays, girls are often more forward than boys and make it really difficult to resist their advances. A Mighty Warrior stands firm and resorts to his training to maintain his honor. Respect yourself and the girl even if she does not value an honorable relationship. Do not fall for the flattery that comes from her lips or the moves her body makes to tempt you.

Compare the stories of Samson and Joseph. Samson was chosen by God from conception. He was born to be used by God to deliver Israel out of the hands of the Philistines. (Judges 13:5) Samson was so strong that he killed a lion with his bare hands and slaughtered thirty of his enemies by himself. God's anointing was on him from birth. Yet, he died in dishonor as a captive of the Philistines, the very ones he was to have defeated, because he fell for the seductions of a beautiful woman. You can read this story in Judges, chapters 13-16.

Joseph was also set apart by God to deliver the Israelites. Although he was sold into slavery by his brothers, he chose to focus on God and trust Him in the bad circumstances of life. When Potiphar's wife begged him to go to bed with her, he declared, "How then can I do this great wickedness, and sin against God?" (Genesis 39:9) Then he fled immediately without looking back. Joseph honored God, Potiphar and his wife, as well as himself with his response. Even though Joseph went to prison for the crime he did not commit, he finished strong. He maintained a positive attitude and worked to the best of his ability while in prison. After his release, he became Pharaoh's Prime Minister and saved Egypt, his family, and the Jewish nation from death when famine struck the region. Joseph fulfilled God's purpose for his life through his obedience. Joseph's story is found in Genesis, chapters 37 through 48.

Both Samson and Joseph began life anointed to do great things. Poor choices changed the course of Samson's life to destruction. Wise decisions kept Joseph in God's perfect will even when it appeared to be a disaster. Just like Samson and Joseph, you have choices to make each day. You do not have to fall for the lures of teasing girls. A Mighty Warrior plans his strategy for battle ahead of time. Prepare responses before situations arise. Train your mind and body to flee from trouble. Enlist your buddies to take a stand with you. A united front achieves amazing victories in battle.

But what if you have already crossed the line sexually? You may think it is too late for you. **LIE!** The enemy works extra hard to make you believe you are defeated and have no chance of survival. Stand firm in what your training manual, The Bible, has taught you. With God, it is never too late to repent, ask forgiveness, and begin again. God is in the business of restoring what the enemy has stolen from you. Your heavenly Father

What If? Freedom Ministries ~ P.O. Box 470252 ~ Tulsa, Oklahoma 74147-0252 ~ 918-249-FREE (3733) ~ www.whatifministires.com

41

does not condone sex outside of marriage, but He always forgives when you ask sincerely for His forgiveness. In fact, right now would be a good time to ask God to forgive you for any sexual sins you have committed. Take a few minutes to search your heart and allow God to speak to you about wrong behavior. This may be painful and hard to admit, but the Truth sets you free. Stop now and ask for His forgiveness. Write down this date in the margin. When the devil tries to tell you that you can't be forgiven for what you have done, go back to this page and tell him he's a liar!

An important part of forgiveness is repentance. God loves you and meets you right where you are. You were forgiven when Jesus died on the cross. You were reconciled to, made right with, God when you asked Him for His forgiveness. Your part, repentance, requires a change in your behavior. Confess your sins to God and find a trusted, godly man to hold you accountable to change your behavior. This is not a quick or easy assignment. But you cannot win the battle on your own. Do not fear ridicule or shame. A true friend will walk beside you and help you carry your battle gear when necessary. Remember, fear comes from the enemy. It is one of his most powerful weapons against you. Be wise and fear not. The courageous soldier may feel afraid, but he does the right thing anyway. That is real bravery.

Another topic promoted by pornography is homosexuality and lesbianism. Watching this type of porn has been the downfall of many men. It plants ideas and images that challenge your manhood. The Bible speaks strongly about homosexuality calling it an abomination to the Lord. In the beginning of Genesis, The Bible narrates the story of creation. In Genesis 1:27 (NIV) it states, "So God created man in His own image, in the image of God He created him; male **and** female He created them." God did not create a unisex Adam and Eve. Adam was all male, and Eve was all female. Before Adam and Eve, God made the earth and heavens, plants, and animals. The plants and animals had seeds to reproduce and replenish the earth. Like the plants and animals, Adam was created with his seed, sperm. Until Eve was created, he had no place to plant his seed. Adam was a warrior just like you. One of the first commands God gave him was to be fruitful and subdue the earth. That is a challenge to you today. Be fruitful spiritually now and physically after marriage. Your mission to subdue the earth is to take command over your circumstances, your hormones, your attitudes, your words, and your actions. Go on the offensive and take control of your battlefield. Be the man God has called you to be.

Satan uses many and varied tactics to try to defeat you. Technology and the internet can be used for good or evil. But you must be aware of your enemy and how cleverly he tricks those he is fighting. Virtual role-playing games are popular online. Many teens who are dissatisfied with their lives turn to this fantasy world where they create the "person" they want to be. Their avatar is their new person in the virtual world. This virtual person becomes the exciting, poplar, "loved" character who may become a refuge from true reality. In balance the games can be fun; but out of balance, role-playing games are addictive and dangerous. Internet bullying is another serious issue on the net. It attacks unsuspecting teens who put too much detailed information about themselves on their web pages. Not everyone who goes to your site has good intentions. There are

What If? Freedom Ministries ~ P.O. Box 470252 ~ Tulsa, Oklahoma 74147-0252 ~ 918-249-FREE (3733) ~ www.whatifministires.com

42

those who would use your information to harm you or even blackmail you. Set boundaries for yourself on the internet, and limit the amount of time you spend there.

Sexual predators love the internet. You can never know for sure with whom you are chatting online. Pedophiles study and practice how to sound like a teenager online; and they are good at it. Sexual predators often share information about their targets with other predators to network to weaken their prey. They are good at discovering weaknesses and filling emotional needs of those they lure into their web. Young people do not stand a chance against a coalition of sexual attackers. Your best defense would be never to go into chat rooms and to message only those that you know personally. And NEVER meet someone in person that you have known only via the internet.

The story of Justin should be a lesson to all who frequent the internet. He was a popular, honor student in middle school when he bought a webcam to expand his group of friends. In a matter of hours after using his webcam on his computer, he was contacted by male pedophiles. At first, it all seemed innocent and friendly. Gradually, Justin began to trust his new friends as the relationships developed. **(Be careful about a false sense of security and trust on the net. The anonymity of the internet lures you into the enemy's web and causes you to lower your guard much faster than in a person-to-person meeting.)** In a very short time, one "friend" said he would pay Justin $50.00 if he would take off his shirt while on the webcam. Soon that progressed to masturbating on camera. Several years of male prostitution followed before Justin escaped the prison of child pornography and sex trade. Justin was a good student with many friends who was manipulated by predators for their selfishness and profit at Justin's expense. You are fighting a smart and powerful enemy. Do not underestimate him. Educate yourself about the devil's strategies and do not cross into his territory. Drill into your mind that God is so much smarter and more powerful than the devil. Use His wisdom and discernment to defeat your enemy.

The advent of social media added a whole new dimension to the battle for your mind. It is an amazing place to share with friends. It also has a dark side. If you have your own web page, be careful what kind of information you are giving out about yourself. Not everyone who visits your web site has honorable intentions. Even your peers may use this format against you to bully, spread unfounded rumors, and ruin your good reputation. Predators prowl through sites looking for information about young people. Unintentionally, thousands of teens provide enough data for anyone who is interested to "befriend" them and find where they live. For example, your page may list your favorite activities, school subjects, foods, sports, etc. A predator then can use that information to make contact and pretend to like the same things you do. Comments about school and social activities often give clues to where you live. Pictures may have landmarks or names in the background that can easily be traced. A determined predator needs few clues and very little time to find his prey. Many sexual predators travel all over the country to stalk and meet their victims. Be very careful what information you put out there. Check out all those who want to be your friends. You cannot be too careful. A good soldier remains alert at all times and is not fooled into thinking "it will never happen to me."

What If? Freedom Ministries ~ P.O. Box 470252 ~ Tulsa, Oklahoma 74147-0252 ~ 918-249-FREE (3733) ~ www.whatifministires.com

43

As mentioned earlier in this chapter, the Internet has opened a whole new world for the promotion of pornography and sexual sin. You, Mighty Warrior, are the target of the porn industry. But God is bigger than the devil and all his evil plans for you. God has a good plan for you and offers help to win the war for your integrity. God created sex and said it is good. It is normal to struggle with your sexual identity and the temptations all around you. But you do not have to give in. You were made to be a warrior, a mighty man of God. Never underestimate the power of God in you!

Study the following scriptures and allow God to speak His Truth into your mind.

Proverbs 6:23-26

_____

_____

Matthew 5:27-28

_____

_____

1 Corinthians 6:9-10 & 18-20

_____

_____

Titus 2:11-12

_____

_____

James 1:13-15

_____

_____

What If? Freedom Ministries ~ P.O. Box 470252 ~ Tulsa, Oklahoma 74147-0252 ~ 918-249-FREE (3733) ~ www.whatifministires.com

44

2 Peter 1:5-8

_____

_____

1 John 2:16-17

_____

_____

Memory Verse – Romans 6:12-14 (NIV)

Therefore do not let sin reign in your mortal body so that you obey its evil desires. Do not offer the parts of your body to sin, as instruments of wickedness, but rather offer yourselves to God, as those who have been brought from death to life; and offer the parts of your body to him as instruments of righteousness. For sin shall not be your master, because you are not under law, but under grace.

Thinking Points

Pornography is no big deal. Every guy looks at least once. Do you agree or disagree? Make your case.

_____

_____

_____

What safeguards do you have in place for internet safety and security?

_____

_____

_____

What If? Freedom Ministries ~ P.O. Box 470252 ~ Tulsa, Oklahoma 74147-0252 ~ 918-249-FREE (3733) ~ www.whatifministires.com

45

What tactics do you use to fight your battle against pornography?

_____

_____

_____

List five tactics you will use to protect the honor of the girls you may date.

_____

_____

_____

_____

_____

What If?
God provides sexual boundaries to protect you and set you free to be the man of God He has created you to be.

What If? Freedom Ministries ~ P.O. Box 470252 ~ Tulsa, Oklahoma 74147-0252 ~ 918-249-FREE (3733) ~ www.whatifministires.com

46

Chapter 5
Know Your Enemy

For our struggle is not against flesh and blood, but against the rulers,
against the authorities, against the powers of this dark world and
against the spiritual forces of evil in the heavenly realms.
Ephesians 6:12 (NIV)

The greatest military leaders in history studied their opponents until they knew the enemy thoroughly and understood how his mind worked. You must do the same if you are to fight the battle effectively. In the war for integrity, who is the enemy? Many will say it is parents, teachers, most adults, or anyone with authority over you. Please understand that they are not your enemy! The adults in your life really do want you to enjoy your life and protect you from harm. Their goal is not to keep you from having fun! Quite the opposite, the adults in your life want to help you avoid wrong choices that may result in serious, life-changing consequences.

This is a spiritual battle that can only be won in the spirit world. Satan is your enemy. You cannot see him with your physical eyes, but the evidence of his work is everywhere – pain, sorrow, deceit, jealousy, pride, anger, and the list goes on. The devil will use anything and anyone to destroy you. You must learn to recognize this evidence and develop tactics to evade and counter-attack. Satan is powerful and very tricky, but God is so much more powerful. The devil wants you to believe he has more power than he actually does. His plan is to discourage you and to destroy God's perfect plan for you. This is psychological warfare.

Your enemy has a plan to demolish you. He wants to flood your mind with fear and doubt. You do not have to buy into that tactic. Read Isaiah 43:1-3 to hear God's counterattack. Those words are powerful weapons at your disposal. The devil also works to distract you so that your perspective is not God's. He works diligently to make you focus on your problems, circumstances, and the small irritants of life instead of on God's enormous love and plan for you. Use Romans 8:1-6 to reinforce your position with Father God.

Another part of psychological warfare is the enemy's desire to mess with your mind, body, and emotions. He is devious at planting thoughts and roadblocks to weaken each area. Do not fall for his tactics. Pull out your Sword and study scriptures like Mark 14:32-36 that show how Jesus even suffered attacks from the adversary. The devil still chooses strategic times and methods to hit you while you are vulnerable. Be aware of when you are most at risk – just before a battle and/or breakthrough and just after a victory. The longer the fight the more your enemy will push to wear you down so that you will grow weary of the battle and give in to fatigue and frustration. You must continue to choose what is right no matter how difficult the battle.

What If? Freedom Ministries ~ P.O. Box 470252 ~ Tulsa, Oklahoma 74147-0252 ~ 918-249-FREE (3733) ~ www.whatifministires.com

47

The greater your opposition, the harder you have to fight. The harder you fight, the better warrior you become. Do not be discouraged by the enemy, but engage the battle with confidence in who you are in Christ. You plus God can conquer any foe. Focus on His strength in you, not yours as you maximize your strengths and minimize your weaknesses. The devil will tempt you wherever he sees a weak spot. He fights dirty, so you must be alert and prepared at all times. Do not listen to your emotions. What you feel is not necessarily the Truth. God's Word is. You may feel like punching someone our. God says, "Have patience; the battle belongs to the Lord." You may feel like staying in bed all day to hide from your problems. God says, "You and I together can tackle any problem headed your way." You may feel that being intimate with your girlfriend will make all your troubles go away. God says, "Seek intimacy with Me. I will provide all the love that you need." Emotions lie and open the door to all kinds of problems. Learn to make choices based on God's Word instead of feelings. Out of love for Him, choose to obey and yield to His instruction. He is waiting for you to be available to Him and to be willing to listen to His still small voice and obey. You do not have to be perfect, just willing.

You were made to be a Warrior. You will have struggles and tribulation your entire life, but God also made you to be an overcomer. Jesus has overcome every sin and every problem for you. (John 16:33) That's a pretty amazing thought. All you have to do is apply His tactics and weapons in your daily battles. That does not mean that the enemy will give up. Satan wants to control you, and he is especially good at using your emotions to do so. If he can gain a foothold in your mind and emotions, he can control your behavior. If he can control your behavior, he can steal your destiny. Use The Word to be victorious over Satan's psychological warfare tactics and secure God's great plan and destiny designed just for you. God is on your side and has planned your victory. Study the devil's tactics to take advantage of his weaknesses while you maximize your strengths.

Deception in warfare is used to divert forces away from the actual strike force. Satan is skilled in deception. His very nature is deceit. He will do anything to distract you from a relationship with the Creator of the Universe. Reconnaissance is a major part of preparation for battle. Today satellites, aerial photography, human intelligence on the ground, drones, and other means of information gathering provide commanders and planning staff up-to-the-minute data on the capabilities of enemy forces. Assessing the strengths and weaknesses of your enemy is necessary in your proper deployment of forces. Never underestimate the enemy, but do not be intimidated by his apparent strengths. Everyone has weaknesses, especially Satan. Let's look at your enemy and learn how to beat him at his own game.

Examine two of his names – Satan and the devil. The name Satan means adversary. He is the opponent of God according to Job 1:6-12 and 2:1-7. The name "devil" comes from the word "diabolos" which means an accuser, a slanderer. The enemy constantly accuses you of wrong-doing and brings your failings even to the throne of God. But, praise God, Jesus is your advocate, your lawyer, who pleads your case before His Father. You are well represented. 1 John 3:8 (NIV) states that "He who does what is sinful is of the devil,

What If? Freedom Ministries ~ P.O. Box 470252 ~ Tulsa, Oklahoma 74147-0252 ~ 918-249-FREE (3733) ~ www.whatifministires.com

48

because the devil has been sinning from the beginning. The reason the Son of God appeared was to destroy the devil's work." Scripture is full of descriptions of Satan and God. Take a few minutes to review the following list that compares Satan to the descriptions of God and the Holy Spirit.

Satan/the devil	God/the Holy Spirit
Adversary 1 Peter 5:8	**Advocate** Hebrews 9:24, Job 16:19
Subtle, sneaky Gen. 3:1-5	**Trustworthy** Psalm 9:10
Murderer, liar John 8:44	**Just and upright** Deuteronomy 32:3-4
Envy, self-seeking James 3:14-16	**Faithful** Psalm 31:5, 1 John 1:9
Deceiver Rev. 20:10, 2 John 7	**Truth** John 16:13, 14:6
Enemy Ephesians 1:6	**Friend** Matt. 11:19, John 15:15

This short list provides insight into your true enemy and weapons available from God for your use. You have no reason to fear the devil because God is on your side. Utilize His weapons to fight this war. (For more names and descriptions, see the list at the end of this chapter.)

Deception is one of Satan's most powerful tools. You must be aware of the lies of the devil regarding sexuality. Remember, sexual integrity is not just avoiding sexual intercourse before marriage. Purity includes your body, mind, and spirit. It is God's will that you remain pure in your body, not touching anyone inappropriately anywhere at any time. But the mind and spirit are the bigger issue here. Jesus said that if a man even looks at a woman with lust in his heart, he has committed adultery. (Matthew 5:28) Keeping your thoughts pure, especially in our sex-saturated society, is hard but not impossible. Pornography plays a big part in this. It is everywhere – movies, music videos, commercials, billboards, the mall, television, girls dressed provocatively. Yet, pornography is not about sex. It is consumed with selfishness, control, lust, and power. It involves the mind. Keeping your spirit holy and upright before God gives Him permission to help you keep your mind and body holy. You must be pure in mind, body, and spirit.

What If? Freedom Ministries ~ P.O. Box 470252 ~ Tulsa, Oklahoma 74147-0252 ~ 918-249-FREE (3733) ~ www.whatifministires.com

49

So, what are some of the devil's lies? Number one, sex is a four-letter word. Satan would have you believe that sex is dirty and sinful, something to be manipulated selfishly. It is just the opposite. Sex, in the context of marriage, is an amazing gift from God. Look at Genesis 2:25. After God created Eve from the rib of Adam, Adam said, "Whoa, you are hot!" Or something like that. The man and his wife were both naked, and they felt no shame. Only after the slippery snake convinced Eve to disobey God (and Adam went along) did nakedness become a shameful thing, perverted by Satan and man. Sex, the way God intended, is a spiritual as well as a physical union between a man and his wife. It is a symbol of the love of Christ for His bride, the church. Sexual intercourse between the husband and wife is a sacred act, beautiful and holy. The devil is a master at taking what God meant for good and turning it into something sinful. He is the master of lies. Refuse to be fooled by our culture that embraces Satan's philosophy of "if it feels good, do it."

The next lie is that you are alone in your struggles, the only one ever to have felt the way you do or to have done such "horrible things." Consider masturbation, for example. It is a major part of pornography and a big issue for guys. A survey of college men found that 88% of them had masturbated at least once. You are NOT alone when it comes to sexual temptations! This does not mean that masturbation is acceptable just because so many men are tempted in this area. That is just another lie of the enemy.

The Word says that "no temptation has seized you except what it is common to man." (1 Corinthians 10:13 NIV) That means you are NOT alone. Lustful desires and fantasies are part of every man's battle. Feeling alone creates the desire to hide your thoughts and actions. Don't fall for the lies that no one would believe you if you told them what you are suffering or that everyone will make fun of you if you are honest. Go back to The Bible. There is nothing new on this earth. You are NOT alone. Sharing your temptations and failings with another trustworthy believer is a huge step toward conquering the enemy. The Truth sets you free. There is strength in numbers. Satan has hordes of demons to tempt and fight against you. But God is mighty in you. Take courage as you fight alongside God and other warriors as Leviticus 26:8 (NIV) says "Five of you will chase a hundred, and a hundred of you will chase ten thousand, and your enemies will fall by the sword before you." Do not allow the feelings of pride, unworthiness, fear, shame, guilt, low self-esteem, or any other emotion the devil hurls at you prevent you from uniting with others in your battle for excellence.

An exit poll taken at a Promise Keepers event revealed that well over 50% of those attending had viewed pornography during the week leading up to the conference. If you struggle with pornography, YOU ARE NOT ALONE. If you are struggling with the temptation of sexual activity, YOU ARE NOT ALONE. Don't let the fear of thinking you are the only one with these temptations trick you into secrecy. The temptation is not sin; don't act on it. Everyone is tempted. The problem occurs when temptation crosses the line into sinful behavior. Get help. Pray; talk to a trusted, godly man; never suffer in silence. Trust your warrior buddies to support you in the battle.

What If? Freedom Ministries ~ P.O. Box 470252 ~ Tulsa, Oklahoma 74147-0252 ~ 918-249-FREE (3733) ~ www.whatifministires.com

50

Studies of Christian teens indicate that many have experienced sexual intercourse. They have also engaged in fondling of breasts, genitals, or other sexual exploits. Make no mistake, these are all dangerous and sinful actions, and if you are participating in this type of activity or even thinking about it, please go to a trusted adult who will give you godly advice and support. Remember, YOU ARE NOT ALONE. Think about the other side. Many more have **NOT** been sexually active. You are not the only one who desires to live a virtuous life.

In boot camp soldiers are conditioned to depend on their unit for their lives. That means no secrets. Survival depends on that. Be open and honest with each other. You are not alone in your struggles. You are human and forgiven, not perfect. But do not allow grace and forgiveness to become an excuse for you to go ahead and sin. That's not what this is about. And don't follow along with the crowd and say it's ok because everybody else is doing it. That is just another lie of the enemy. If "everyone" does it, it is all right. **LIE!** Be tolerant; adjust to the "progress" of modern society. **LIE!** Choose to follow Truth!

God will not condemn you for your past. Have the courage to come out into the light. It is never too late to change. God gives back what the enemy has stolen from you. Isolation and shame are tools Satan uses to keep you in the darkness which prohibits God from helping you. That is where Phil made his biggest mistake. The shame and guilt were so overpowering that the fear of rejection kept him trapped in the pit of pornography for 40 years. Realizing you are not alone should encourage you to reach out for help. James 5:16 teaches that you should confess your sins to each other so that you will be healed. Satan tempts you to sin and then condemns you for acting on his lie. God is always ready to forgive, forget, and restore you. If Phil had believed that Truth in the early years of his addiction to pornography, he might not have kept it hidden so long. He suffered most of his life because he believed the lie that he was the only one and that no one could love him because of his secret shame. YOU ARE NOT ALONE! You cannot go so far that God's arm is not able to pull you back into His embrace. Satan condemns you and makes you feel guilt and shame. God will convict you about sin in your life, but He does it out of His great love for you. Think about this.

Condemnation – I sin; run from God
Conviction – I sin; run to God

Another lie to consider is that "it" will go away in marriage. Wrong! Most teens we recently interviewed expressed the idea that pornography is okay if you do not have a steady girlfriend or are not married. In addition, pre-marital sexual activity is acceptable in modern society. They felt certain that once they marry, pornography and consequences of fooling around will no longer be a part of their lives. That is a lie! Phil personally believed that lie. But his pornography use increased each year he was married and nearly cost him his family. Here's the deal. Pornography or sexual addiction is just like substance abuse. The satisfaction level keeps creeping higher and higher. You always need more to satisfy your lustful passions.

What If? Freedom Ministries ~ P.O. Box 470252 ~ Tulsa, Oklahoma 74147-0252 ~ 918-249-FREE (3733) ~ www.whatifministires.com

51

King David's involvement with pornography and sexual sin created lifelong problems for him. When he noticed Bathsheba bathing on her rooftop, rather than turn away immediately, he stared at her body and lusted after her. After he slept with her and she became pregnant, he used his authority as king to send her husband Uriah to the frontlines of battle ensuring his death. David was married during this entire affair and murdered to hide his secret, adultery. It wasn't until the prophet Nathan confronted David about his sin that he repented and sought God's forgiveness. He was forgiven, but David's reign as king was troubled with family problems and constant relationship issues. And yet, how does God describe King David? God calls him "a man after His own heart." (Acts 13:22) Actions have consequences, but you can always be restored to a right relationship with Abba Father. Better to follow Truth than to enjoy momentary pleasures with long-lasting, negative consequences. Now is the time to deal with pornography and sexual temptations, not after you are married. Preserve yourself for your future wife and reap positive rewards.

Fear of rejection is another powerful weapon the devil uses. Peer pressure is a massive force in the lives of teens. Many are afraid that if they do not look at pornography, make sexual advances, and even have sex before marriage they will be laughed at, ridiculed, and never have a girl interested in them. Feeling rejected can tear you apart. Everyone wants to feel loved and accepted. That is normal. God created that desire in each of us. However, Satan is a master at twisting something good – love and acceptance – into fear that creates wrong behavior. Be assured that God loves and accepts you just the way you are. Sometimes that is easy to say and believe in your mind. It can be difficult to know it deep down inside when it appears that no one cares or understands.

One of the tactics used to break prisoners of war is to tell them over and over and over again that no one cares about them, their wives have left them for other men, everyone has abandoned them. It is a very effective method to discourage and defeat POWs. The devil created this cruelty and uses it in his effort to demoralize you. When the enemy lobs a grenade of rejection in your direction, focus on how much God and others believe in you. Visualize the Holy Spirit diving on the grenade and covering it with His body to protect you from harm. You are loved not only by God but also by family, teachers, pastors, and true friends. A real friend, your soldiers in arms, stands with you through good and bad. Yes, you will fail and disappoint those around you. They will let you down sometimes, too. But love forgives. 1 Corinthians 13:4-8 is often used in marriage ceremonies. But those words are really powerful for you right now. Think about this from The Message Bible.

> Love never gives up
> Love cares more for others than for self
> Love doesn't want what it doesn't have
> Love doesn't strut
> Doesn't have a swelled head
> Doesn't force itself on others
> Isn't always "me first"
> Doesn't fly off the handle

What If? Freedom Ministries ~ P.O. Box 470252 ~ Tulsa, Oklahoma 74147-0252 ~ 918-249-FREE (3733) ~ www.whatifministires.com

52

Doesn't keep score of the sins of others
Doesn't revel when others grovel
Takes pleasure in the flowering of truth
Puts up with anything
Trusts God always
Always looks for the best
Never looks back but keeps going to the end

Do not linger on alien thoughts. Satan is a patient enemy. He knows the longer you think about his deceptions, the more likely you are to believe and to act on them. Give no thought to tricks like "only one time can't hurt," "everybody does it," "did God really tell you...," "you'll look really stupid if...," "if you want to be popular...," "nobody gives a rip about you," "you are worth nothing," etc. Satan loves to play with your mind. Prepare responses to these mental attacks in advance. Shout the Truth! Your best reinforcements are The Bible and a circle of godly friends. Dress for battle and be prepared to fight like a warrior.

With hormones raging in your body, you may feel that obedience to God's Word to remain an honorable warrior is impossible. LIE! You should be seeing the pattern of lies by now. The enemy does not care if you read The Bible or go to church. As long as he can convince you that you cannot put into practice what you are learning, his tactics are paying off. Your best defense is a good offense. Go on the offensive by committing to obey God in every area of your life. Of course, the first time you fail, Satan will tell you that it really is impossible to follow God's battle plan. Persevere. Everyone fails in the beginning. Ask forgiveness, seek advice, and press on toward victory. As you make progress, the enemy will fight even harder to distract and defeat you. Train yourself to think of temptations and battles as a sign that you are doing something right and approaching victory. Remember, God is right in the thick of battle with you. You will always have battles and pain. Anything worth doing will be difficult before it becomes easy. Choose to do the right thing even when it feels wrong.

Here's an important lesson. The pain of disobedience is much worse than the pain of obedience. A huge challenge for all warriors is to understand that the pain of obedience is a good, healing pain. Think of it as the pain of surgery to remove a cancer from your body. Surgery is the healthy option, for without it you will die. Obedience is your healthy choice; a little pain now prevents the "cancer" that could infect your entire body. Dying to self (selfish desires) hurts at first, but that discipline yields peace and confidence in the long run. That enables you to fight your battle without regrets. Your pain of obedience is the opposite of the pain of regret that Phil experienced living in his dark world of pornography.

The good news is that you do not have to suffer the pain of disobedience or regret. It is your choice. You can follow your own path that leads to destruction or pursue your Commander-in-Chief and enjoy the spoils of victory. God prepared an awesome experience, the sexual desire for your bride, for you before you were born. The discipline

What If? Freedom Ministries ~ P.O. Box 470252 ~ Tulsa, Oklahoma 74147-0252 ~ 918-249-FREE (3733) ~ www.whatifministires.com

53

of waiting yields awesome results. Don't quit. God never gives up on you. Don't give up on yourself!

Hopefully, you have a better understanding of the devil and his plans of attack now. You must be vigilant at all times. Satan is very clever in this battle and has much experience destroying the lives of young men. He uses half-truths and innuendos to trick you at every turn. Listen to your Commander-in-Chief and obey instantly.

Use the following scriptures to reinforce your understanding of your enemy.

Isaiah 14:12-15

_____

_____

Matthew 4:1-11

_____

_____

John 8:44

_____

_____

John 16:33

_____

_____

2 Corinthians 2:10-11

_____

_____

What If? Freedom Ministries ~ P.O. Box 470252 ~ Tulsa, Oklahoma 74147-0252 ~ 918-249-FREE (3733) ~ www.whatifministires.com

54

2 Corinthians 4:3-4

_____

_____

1 John 3:6-10

_____

_____

1 John 4:4

_____

_____

Memory verse – 1 Peter 5:8-9 (NIV)

Be self-controlled and alert. Your enemy the devil prowls around like a roaring lion looking for someone to devour. Resist him, standing firm in the faith, because you know that your brothers throughout the world are undergoing the same kind of sufferings.

Thinking Points

List some of the tactics the enemy has used against you. How could you have responded more effectively?

_____

_____

_____

What If? Freedom Ministries ~ P.O. Box 470252 ~ Tulsa, Oklahoma 74147-0252 ~ 918-249-FREE (3733) ~ www.whatifministires.com

55

How has Satan used peer pressure against you? List three tactics to counter these attacks.

_____

_____

_____

Write about a time you experienced the pain of obedience. What weapons did Satan use against you? How did you feel when you won the battle?

_____

_____

_____

Who are some friends (peers and adults) that you can enlist as warrior buddies? Put a date next to each name as a deadline to discuss this with them.

_____

_____

_____

What If?
God knows everything about Satan and how he fights and has equipped you for each battle.

What If? Freedom Ministries ~ P.O. Box 470252 ~ Tulsa, Oklahoma 74147-0252 ~ 918-249-FREE (3733) ~ www.whatifministires.com

56

Names and Descriptions of Satan vs. God

Satan/the devil

Accuser of the brethren
Rev. 12:10
Adversary
1 Peter 5:8
Enemy
Matt. 13:39
Evil Spirit
1 Sam. 16:14
Father of Lies
John 8:44
Lying spirit
1 Kings 22:22
Murderer
John 8:44
Power of Darkness
Col. 1:13
Power of the air
Eph. 2:2
Ruler of the darkness of this world
Eph. 6:12
Serpent
Gen. 3:4,14; Rev. 12:9,20:2
Spirit that works in children of disobedience
Eph. 2:2
Tempter
Matt. 4:1-11
God of this world
2 Cor. 4:4
Unclean Spirit
Matt. 12:43
Wicked one
Matt. 13:19,38
Subtle, sneaky
Gen. 3:1-5
Cursed
Gen. 3:14-15
Provokes
1 Chron. 21:1
Thief
Matt. 13:19,38-39

God/the Holy Spirit

Trustworthy
Psalm 9:10
Truth
John 16:13, 14:6
Kindness
Ephesians 1:6
Endures forever
Psalm 135:13
Everlasting light
Isaiah 60:20
Forgiveness
Acts 10:43, Micah 7:18
Sacrifice
Eph. 5:2, 1 John 2:2
Deliverer   Ps 144:2
Romans 11:26, Hebrews 9:14
Friend
Matt. 11:19, John 15:15
Mediator
Hebrews 12:24, 1 Tim 2:5-6
Merciful, gracious
Exodus 34:6-7
Righteous
Isaiah 53:11, Acts 7:52
Strong Savior
Psalm 140:7, Jeremiah 14:8
Father Ps. 103:13-14,17-18
Romans 8:15-16, John 17:11
Immanuel – God with us
Isaiah 7:14
Peace   2 Thess. 3:16, Eph. 2:14
Isaiah 9:6, Romans 16:20
Advocate
Hebrews 9:24, Job 16:19
Victory
Psalm 48:10, Rom. 16:20
Commander of the Lord's Army
Joshua 5:14
Overcomer
Rev. 17:14

What If? Freedom Ministries ~ P.O. Box 470252 ~ Tulsa, Oklahoma 74147-0252 ~ 918-249-FREE (3733) ~ www.whatifministires.com

57

Satan/the devil

Destroy, kill, steal
John 10:10, 1 Cor. 5:4-5

Attacker
Luke 22:31

Murderer, liar
John 8:44

Plant evil ideas
John 13:2,27

Perversion and mischief
Acts 13:10

Darkness
Acts 26:18

Blind minds
2 Cor. 4:4

Beguiler
2 Cor. 11:3

Angel of light
2 Cor. 11:14

Wicked one
1 John 2:13, Matt. 13:19,38

Hinders
1 Thess. 2:18

Lying/Liar
2 Thess. 2:9, 1 John 2:22

Condemnation
1 Tim. 3:6

Fear Lam. 3:46-47
Job 4:14,18:11 Ps 31:13

Snare
1 Tim. 3:7, 2 Tim. 2:26

Arrogant
Prov. 8:13

Devourer
1 Pet. 5:8\

Sinner
1 John3:8

god of this world
2 Cor. 4:4

Unclean spirit
Matt. 12:43

Shame & Guilt
Genesis 3:10-13

Confusion
1 Cor. 14:33

God/the Holy Spirit

Loving Ally
Psalm 144:2

Mighty Warrior
Ps. 45:3-4, 24:8, Isaiah 33:21

Triumphant Sword
Deuteronomy 33:29

Faithful
Psalm 31:5, 1 John 1:9

Love
1 John 4:16

Answers prayers
Genesis 35:3

Great High Priest
Hebrews 4:14-15

Guardian
1 Peter 2:25

Hope
1 Tim. 1:1

Refuge
Nahum 1:7, Ps. 61:2-3

Light Isaiah 9:2
John 8:12, Luke 1:78-79

Hiding place
Psalm 32:7

Strength
Psalm 18:1

Perfect love
1 John 4:18

Protection
John 17:11-12, Ps 18:30

Fortress
Psalm 62:2, Proverbs 18:10

Safety
Psalm 31:2

Holy
Isaiah 8:13, 29:23, Rev. 4:8

Shield
Psalm 3:3

Intercessor
Hebrews 7:25

Power
Jeremiah 10:6

Builder
Hebrews 3:4

What If? Freedom Ministries ~ P.O. Box 470252 ~ Tulsa, Oklahoma 74147-0252 ~ 918-249-FREE (3733) ~ www.whatifministires.com

58

Satan/the devil

Envy, self-seeking
James 3:14-16
Steals the Word
Luke 8:12, Mark 4:15
Oppressor
Acts 10:38
Enemy of righteousness
Acts 13:10 ??
Death
Hebrews 2:14
Bondage/binds
Luke 13:16
Contender
Jude 9
Wrath
Rev. 12:12
Deceiver
Rev. 20:10, 2 John 7

Offense
Matt. 16:23
Betrayer
Luke 22:3-4
Unclean spirit
Matt. 12:43

God/the Holy Spirit

Wisdom
James 3:17-18, Prov. 8:12,14
Comforter
John 14:26
Life
John 1:4-5
Counselor
John 15:26-27, Isaiah 9:6
Just and upright
Deuteronomy 32:3-4
Good
Matt. 7:11, Luke 12:32,
John 10:11,14; James 1:17
3 John 11; Ps. 34:8;86:5
100:5; 107:1;135:3;145:9

Grace
John 1:14; Acts 11:23
Rom. 3:24;5:15
Mercy
Ps. 23:6; 52:8;94:18;119:64
Lam. 3:22-23;Eph. 2:4-5

Help/Helper
Psalm 124:8, Heb. 13:5

What If? Freedom Ministries ~ P.O. Box 470252 ~ Tulsa, Oklahoma 74147-0252 ~ 918-249-FREE (3733) ~ www.whatifministires.com

59

What If? Freedom Ministries ~ P.O. Box 470252 ~ Tulsa, Oklahoma 74147-0252 ~ 918-249-FREE (3733) ~ www.whatifministires.com

60

Chapter 6
Fight to Win

The war for sexual integrity is a long one, a lifelong battle. Many are not willing to enter the war but try to ignore or appease the enemy. Often public opinion turns against completing the battle because it takes so long and sacrifices have to be made. Do you have the will to fight to the end?

In today's culture it seems everyone wants what they want when they want it. Now! There is a microwave mentality – fast food, ATM's, instant communication, etc. People become impatient waiting for the microwave to cook dinner in five minutes. All this speed has conditioned us to expect quick answers and immediate results with little or no effort or inconvenience on our part. If it feels good, do it; and if it causes pain whether physical, mental, or emotional, switch to something else. Patience and perseverance appear to be a thing of the past. However, they must be embraced if you are to win your war.

According to the dictionary, patience is "the will or ability to wait or endure <u>without complaint</u>; steadiness, endurance, or perseverance in performing a task." Patience is not merely waiting; it is waiting well, without complaint. The law requires that you stop when a traffic light turns to red and then wait for it to change to green before entering the intersection. But how do you wait? Do you accelerate as the green light turns to yellow to avoid stopping for that long red light so that you can continue your journey? Do you rev your engine as if you are on the starting line of the Indy 500 while agonizing over the time you are "wasting" sitting still? Driving in traffic is an excellent opportunity to train yourself to have a long-suffering attitude. Traffic signals, other drivers, and construction zones offer multiple opportunities to practice patience in very practical ways.

Patience and perseverance go hand in hand. The dictionary definition of persevere is "to persist in any business or enterprise undertaken; to pursue steadily any design or course once begun; to be steadfast in purpose." You don't quit; you focus on the goal. Thomas Edison invented the light bulb. He was laughed at, and his experiments failed hundreds of times before he was successful. He persevered until he got it right. No matter how many times you may fail, pick yourself up and try again. Persevere. Together patience and perseverance enable you to have a good attitude while you progress through whatever you are doing – however long it may take. God will never require you to do something without giving you the tools to do it. He allows circumstances in your life to train you to proceed with patience and perseverance. Look at the trials and temptations in your life as learning opportunities, tests. You have as many opportunities to take the tests as you need. Of course, the sooner you surrender your will to God's best for you, the faster you pass the tests.

Look at the Israelites. When they came out of Egypt, they faced an eleven-day journey to the Promised Land, the land of milk and honey. In other words, their dream, reward, and God's desire for them were within reach in less than a two weeks' trip. However, they did not practice God's will for them. They were ungrateful, complaining, and

What If? Freedom Ministries ~ P.O. Box 470252 ~ Tulsa, Oklahoma 74147-0252 ~ 918-249-FREE (3733) ~ <u>www.whatifministires.com</u>

61

disobedient. That eleven-day miracle march turned into 40 years of struggling in the desert with only two of the adults of the original group entering the Land of Promise. You determine your destiny by the way you choose. You can act in haste, selfishness, and folly and live in the wilderness for years; or you can choose the harder way initially and fight your war with God's help, patience, and determination. Victory comes faster to those who wait well. That requires self-discipline, teaching yourself to make right choices no matter how hard it may be. To some, discipline is a dirty word. It requires both patience and perseverance because it usually does not develop quickly or easily. Most soldiers do not look back to boot camp as the highlight of their military career. It was full of hard, long, painful days of intense training with drill sergeants screaming orders. However, once in battle every soldier is thankful for all the pain suffered to be able to fight the enemy well. The value gained from the harshness of the trainers becomes a symbol for survival on the battlefield.

God is similar in His preparation for you. He disciplines and instructs you, oftentimes painfully, so that you can fight the enemy well. Hebrews 12:5-11 (MSG) explains that God corrects you because he speaks to you as His son. In part it says, "But God is doing what is best for us, training us to live God's holy best. At the time, discipline isn't much fun. It always feels like it's going against the grain. Later, of course, it pays off handsomely, for it's the well-trained who find themselves mature in their relationship with God." Life is full of choices. Will you choose the quick fix or persevere for God's best for you? Only you can make that decision.

Set your mind to persevere on your course for excellence. This does not mean that you will be perfect just because you decide to be an honorable soldier. It is a daily battle. Thank God, He created a rhythm to life so that each day has 24 hours; and His mercies are new every morning. Each day you get a fresh start. That is something to rejoice about. Accept the fact that you will fail. Perseverance means that each time you fail, you ask for forgiveness and try again and again and again. As long as you are striving to improve, there is nothing wrong with making mistakes. Learn from them.

You are a Mighty Warrior in a battle for your soul. Satan does not play fair or follow the rules of engagement. He fights dirty. In the last chapter you learned how to recognize his tactics. But understanding his methods is not enough. Wishing for victory is not enough. You have to fight. Be prepared for the long haul. Satan is a relentless opponent who never tires of tempting you and leading you toward destruction. Likewise, you must never give up in the battle. Galatians 6:9 (NIV) says, "Let us not become weary in doing good, for at the proper time we will reap a harvest if we do not give up." One of Satan's most effective strategies is to wear down his targets. He has been fighting this battle since he was kicked out of heaven. He enjoys the fight and believes he will win in the end. That is why he is so persistent. He is focused on the final victory, not the present. If he has trouble defeating you outright, he often leaves you alone for a while but always returns when your guard is down. He is sneaky and has studied his opponents. That means he knows you, your weaknesses and strengths. You can believe he will manipulate your weaknesses to defeat you. Be aware of his methods and believe **YOU WILL WIN!**

What If? Freedom Ministries ~ P.O. Box 470252 ~ Tulsa, Oklahoma 74147-0252 ~ 918-249-FREE (3733) ~ www.whatifministires.com

62

A lesson from history is an excellent example of how Satan fights. Adolph Hitler came to power because he was patient in winning the hearts of the German people. He promised them whatever they wanted – plenty of food, shelter, and power. After the humiliation of defeat in World War I, Germany was not only devastated physically from warfare but also demoralized mentally and emotionally. Hitler used this to his advantage. He worked slowly over many years to gain the trust and adoration of the German people, especially the youth who eventually became his soldiers. He came to them as an angel of light, the answer to all their problems and the savior to lead them out of despair. Patiently, he provided for their needs and gradually filled their minds with his propaganda. The German people were desensitized and so blinded by his lies that they would do anything for him. Only when he controlled their minds did the real Hitler reveal himself. By then, most people could not recognize the truth. They believed whatever he told them.

Encouraged by his tyrannical power, Hitler's control of Germany was not enough. Satan, too, is encouraged by little victories in your life. He is never satisfied with a little; he always wants more of you. To feed his lust for more, Hitler invaded one country after another in Europe with minimal resistance. Out of fear and intimidation, entire nations surrendered to the Nazis. They fell to Hitler's armies as the world watched and waited for the Nazis to be satisfied and stop the rampage. Rather than fight, the Allies negotiated with the enemy. Hitler signed treaties never intending to honor them. They were simply a delaying tactic. Hitler had a plan, an evil plan; and he did whatever it took to fulfill his lust for power. That included deception, betrayal of his allies, The Holocaust, and unbelievable cruelty to his own people. Everything he did was calculated to fulfill his plan. If the Third Reich experienced setbacks, he did not give up. He improvised an alternate strategy to achieve his goal – world domination. Hitler provides great insight into your enemy, Satan. Do you see the similarities? Hitler used the tricks of Satan masterfully and almost conquered the world. Fear, intimidation, and negotiation provide fuel and power to your enemy. Do not try to argue or negotiate with the enemy. You will not win. Trust God and focus on the long-term goal. The devil continues to use these tactics in his effort to conquer the world in general and you in particular.

In the first years of World War II, the Allies were no match for Hitler's determination. Millions of innocent people died while the leaders of the free world debated what to do with Hitler. While he was focused and fighting, they were divided and discussing how to avoid war. As they allowed the Nazis to occupy one nation after another, the Allies fell into Hitler's trap. They avoided confrontation hoping the "problem" would go away if they ignored it long enough. Surely, the "problem" would not affect their individual countries. One can only wonder what might have happened had the Allies united and stood up to Hitler at the outset of his offenses. It would have been painful and taken much effort, but The Third Reich could have been defeated in short order with fewer casualties and without the devastation of Europe. Only when Hitler's targets developed the courage and will to unite and fight until victory was achieved did the tide turn. Even then, it took years of bloody battles to defeat the Nazis. It was a long, difficult war. Millions died because people were afraid to confront the enemy at the beginning. Hitler

What If? Freedom Ministries ~ P.O. Box 470252 ~ Tulsa, Oklahoma 74147-0252 ~ 918-249-FREE (3733) ~ www.whatifministires.com

63

persevered and implemented his plan until forced to surrender to the Allies' united, determined assault.

Every time you give into Satan's ploys, you give him ground in your life. Once lost, that ground is extremely difficult to regain. Keeping your ground may be hard, but retaking it is much more difficult. Avoiding confrontation of your temptations and ignoring the enemy and his strategies do not work. That only allows the devil to proceed deeper into your territory. Stand your ground, persevere in the battle. Recognize your enemy and confront the issues in your life each day to avoid the casualties of war – getting hooked on pornography, loosing your virginity, becoming depressed, and many others. Take offensive action against the enemy in the small battles to short circuit Satan's plan for your life. You do not have to be a casualty of war!

Do not make deals with the devil. He promises whatever you want to entice you to follow him and then abandons you once you are in over your head. He is not trustworthy. He depends on your ignorance and lack of will to fight to destroy you, his enemy. And you are his enemy because you are a child of God. When you are tempted to look at just one pornographic picture on the web, stand your ground. If your "friends" tease you because you are a virgin, find real friends. If you have already given ground to Satan, take it back. Determine right now to remain pure from this day forward and save yourself for your future bride. Fight the thoughts that the devil plants in your mind. You do not have to give in. The battle is long but not impossible to win. Take one day at a time. Replace wrong thinking with godly advice. Listen to your Commander-in-Chief. Remember His tough love and discipline are for your good and protection. Satan is called the angel of light because he tempts you with seemingly good and pleasurable treats. They are tricks. Do not give in to him. He is a voracious enemy, and the more ground you give him the more he will take. Fight back! You cannot be a pacifist in this war. You can never appease Satan. He will not stop until you are destroyed. But God gives you life and the power not only to fight but also to win the war – if you persevere.

Your strategy must be to focus on the long-term goal – integrity for a lifetime. Never give up. Persevere. Be patient as God teaches you His tactics to engage the enemy. Satan may leave you alone for a while, but he will return to torment you the moment you give him the opportunity. If he was brazen enough to tempt Jesus during His ministry on Earth, the devil will do all in his power to entice you to sin. After Jesus resisted the enemy in the wilderness, The Bible says that Satan left Him until a more convenient time would come. That describes the devil's persistence pretty well. Jesus was triumphant over Satan in the wilderness, yet the devil did not admit defeat, only a minor setback. Be vigilant against the enemy's sneak attacks. Persevere, persevere, persevere! God will give you the strength for each battle. When you are weak, He shows Himself strong in you. God has a great advantage over the enemy. He knows everything. He is all powerful. He is with you every second of every day. What better comrade in arms could you hope for! He is in your battle for the long haul. Plus, you have a mighty army surrounding you with not only family and friends but angels stationed all around you. You can't loose with those odds.

What If? Freedom Ministries ~ P.O. Box 470252 ~ Tulsa, Oklahoma 74147-0252 ~ 918-249-FREE (3733) ~ www.whatifministires.com

64

Use these scriptures and what God reveals to you as reinforcements in your battle.

2 Chronicles 16:9

_____

_____

1 Corinthians 9:24-27

_____

_____

2 Corinthians 4:7-9

_____

_____

Galatians 6:9

_____

_____

Philippians 2:13

_____

_____

Philippians 3:14

_____

_____

What If? Freedom Ministries ~ P.O. Box 470252 ~ Tulsa, Oklahoma 74147-0252 ~ 918-249-FREE (3733) ~ www.whatifministires.com

65

2 Timothy 2:3-7

_____

_____

Hebrews 12:1-3

_____

_____

James 1:12

_____

_____

Memory verse – Romans 8:37-39 (NIV)

In all these things we are more than conquerors through Him who loved us. For I am convinced that neither death nor life, neither angels nor demons, neither the present nor the future, nor any powers, neither height nor depth, nor anything else in all creation, will be able to separate us from the love of God that is in Christ Jesus our Lord.

Thinking Points

Write about an area of your life where you need more patience. What are three things that you can do to gain patience in this aspect of your life?

_____

_____

_____

What If? Freedom Ministries ~ P.O. Box 470252 ~ Tulsa, Oklahoma 74147-0252 ~ 918-249-FREE (3733) ~ www.whatifministires.com

66

Are persistence and perseverance strengths or weaknesses in you? Explain. What can you do to develop greater perseverance in your life?

_____

_____

_____

List examples of how the enemy has persistently attacked you. How do you fight back?

_____

_____

_____

Describe an instance where God helped you persevere in a difficult temptation. (If you can't think of one, write about a temptation where you failed. How would you handle that differently now?)

_____

_____

_____

Write three points of your battle plan for victory. Put the desired date of implementation next to each one.

_____

_____

_____

What If?
God has given you the will to fight to the finish.

What If? Freedom Ministries ~ P.O. Box 470252 ~ Tulsa, Oklahoma 74147-0252 ~ 918-249-FREE (3733) ~ www.whatifministires.com

67

What If? Freedom Ministries ~ P.O. Box 470252 ~ Tulsa, Oklahoma 74147-0252 ~ 918-249-FREE (3733) ~ www.whatifministires.com

68

Chapter 7
Honorable Soldier

God's desire is for you to be a Mighty Warrior, a man of honor. The way you think about and treat the opposite sex powerfully affects your ability to be that Mighty Warrior. Since men are visually stimulated, it is critical that you protect your eyes from sinning by looking at girls with less than honorable thoughts. Ah yes, thoughts. You must control your mind, your thought life, to remain pure for your future wife. That is no easy task. But it is possible with God's help. This chapter will stretch your thinking about how you can relate to girls with honor and respect.

In His wisdom, God created man and woman. He made them very different from each other – and not just physically. Whereas what you see affects you quickly and deeply, girls are relational beings who need to feel genuinely loved. Men respond to situations the opposite of women in many cases. That is not wrong, just different. During the teen years, it will serve you well to focus on God's plan for your life and what He wants you to do in regards to the opposite sex. This is very different from what our culture teaches and models for today's teens.

How would a man of integrity treat young ladies? The first word that comes to mind is "respect." A godly man respects God, himself, and others. If you respect God, then you will want to honor Him with your thoughts and actions. You will study His Word to know what He has to say about your relationships with the opposite sex. God knows your mind can deceive you and cause you to stumble. That's why Jesus said that if a man looks at a woman with lust in his heart, he has committed adultery. Your mind is a powerful weapon in the war for integrity. Train yourself to think godly thoughts when you are around girls. Those thoughts begin in you. Respect yourself; like yourself. There is a healthy way to love yourself and not be selfish in that love. Once you value yourself, you can respect and care about others the way God intended. Love your future wife enough to wait for God's choice of a mate for you.

In our society, that can be difficult. The prevailing attitude is that you should be "trying out" as many girls as possible in the dating game. Girls are not an item on a shelf to be sampled and tossed aside if they don't meet your desires or you tire of them. Honor the girls in your life. One of the greatest areas of temptation in teens' lives involves the subject of dating. This is a fairly recent acceptable form of social activity that demands serious thought and study. You cannot find any reference to dating in The Bible. Arranged marriages and betrothals were common. Throughout history, women had chaperones whenever in male company until they were married. That is the exception rather than the rule today. However, some couples have committed not even to hold hands until their wedding and to share their first kiss at the marriage altar. Although that is a great option for some, it may seem a bit extreme for you. What is important is that you remain pure not only physically but also emotionally until marriage. Physically, do not dishonor yourself or the girl you are with by crossing the line – from touching inappropriately, passionate kissing, oral sex, to sexual intercourse. Contrary to popular

What If? Freedom Ministries ~ P.O. Box 470252 ~ Tulsa, Oklahoma 74147-0252 ~ 918-249-FREE (3733) ~ www.whatifministires.com

69

belief, you are not pure and not a virgin if you have abstained only from vaginal intercourse. You may be "technically" a virgin but not emotionally. God's desire is for you to respect and value your body and the body of the girls in your life.

God's laws are not to keep you from enjoying your life. They are to protect you, physically and emotionally, to give you deep joy and fulfillment. Physical restraint is hard, but emotional integrity can seem even more complicated. How do you determine if you have violated emotional boundaries? Having friends of the opposite sex is good. When you think of girls as sex objects or even possible wives, you are emotionally involved. Each relationship with a girl that goes beyond friendship is an emotional involvement. You are giving away a part of your heart and taking a part of hers. Think about how much of your heart you want to give away before you marry. Are you a one-woman man? Do you want a one-man woman? Pray and ask the Holy Spirit to show you what boundaries He wants you to set for your relationships.

The world sees male-female relationships in its own way. Our culture encourages young people to experiment and go for the gusto at earlier and earlier ages. God's perspective is the opposite of what the world expects. Let's compare the two viewpoints. Hold up your hand to represent the world's view on relationships. Each digit stands for a level of a relationship. Your thumb is number one in importance on society's scale. Look at the picture on the next page.

What If? Freedom Ministries ~ P.O. Box 470252 ~ Tulsa, Oklahoma 74147-0252 ~ 918-249-FREE (3733) ~ www.whatifministires.com

70

Five Levels of Relationships

World View

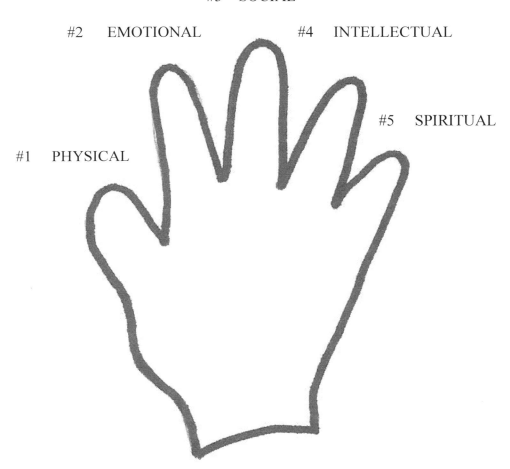

#3   SOCIAL

#2   EMOTIONAL   #4   INTELLECTUAL

#5   SPIRITUAL

#1   PHYSICAL

What If? Freedom Ministries ~ P.O. Box 470252 ~ Tulsa, Oklahoma 74147-0252 ~ 918-249-FREE (3733) ~ www.whatifministires.com

71

This hand represents the world's priorities in relationships. According to this view, the first level is the physical aspect. You see a girl and are physically attracted to her. How do you look at her? Do you stare at her breasts and then look her up and down? That is often promoted as the manly thing to do in our society. Hollywood would have you believe that every woman is a target for man's lustful thoughts and behaviors. The physical side of the relationship is all that matters. It can be easy to move from eye contact, to holding hands, a kiss on the cheek, to passionate kissing in a very short time. When you reach this stage of sexual activity, new desires awaken in both of you. Once you have crossed this line, the progression is similar to sliding down an icy hill. Petting with clothes on, experimenting with nudity, and trying oral sex are often close behind. Many expect to have sexual intercourse on the first date. The world's view encourages people to do whatever they want whenever they want. Commitment is not an issue. Live for the moment and ignore possible consequences like pregnancy, guilt, depression, or STDs (sexually transmitted diseases). As a result, teens are more and more involved with dangerous behavior. Open mouthed kissing, fondling genitals, and oral sex have become popular activities. Even teens who have committed to save themselves for marriage participate in these and rationalize their behavior by saying that as long as they do not have vaginal penetration sexual intercourse, they are still virgins. What a masterful lie of the devil our culture has believed. Mighty man of God, believe Truth!

The second level of relationship according to our culture is emotional. This may not seem like a big deal to you since men, in general, tend not to focus on their feelings. Boys can count their emotions on one hand whereas girls need a calculator to keep track of everything going on inside of them. Expressing emotions is not bad, but you cannot allow them to control you. God created emotions. You just express yours very differently from the opposite sex. Not wrong, just different. But you do need to understand that difference. Guys, because of their emotional make-up, girls are susceptible to what you say. You may casually tell a girl that she is beautiful or that you love her. Be careful. Those words are powerful in a girl's mind. She is influenced by your conversation. Don't toy with her emotions.

Hormones definitely affect your emotions. At puberty your body and mind are awakening sexually. Overnight you can change from thinking girls are disgusting to believing you can't live without the girl of your dreams. This time of transition can pose some of the greatest challenges of your life. Allowing your hormones and emotions to control you can create huge problems for you to overcome. Develop a strategy to short circuit those emotions especially in the area of sexuality and your relationship with girls. Purposely set boundaries for yourself and enforce them. Avoid getting into situations where temptation can overtake you and your emotions entice you to violate your boundaries for godly behavior. Group dating is safer than single dating. Watching a romantic movie with a girl alone at home is a dangerous activity. Parking your car in an isolated place to "talk" is an invitation to cross the line physically and emotionally.

Even if you avoid physical contact with a girl, the emotional side of the relationship can cause heartache. Each time you sweet talk a girl or encourage her to flirt with you, you are taking a piece of her heart. Since girls are so much more relational than boys, it is

What If? Freedom Ministries ~ P.O. Box 470252 ~ Tulsa, Oklahoma 74147-0252 ~ 918-249-FREE (3733) ~ www.whatifministires.com

72

easy for them to think a relationship with you is more than you intend. Do not give away pieces of your heart, and do not play with any girl's emotions.

The third level of relationships in the world view is social. Notice the social side comes after the physical and emotional damage has been done. Socially, you enjoy doing things together and are not embarrassed to be seen with each other in public. You may introduce the girl to your family and friends for them to get to know her also. You are not necessarily asking for their approval but want them to meet her. The two of you spend time together with family and friends so that you interact as a couple with others. You are checking out how the two of you fit together in the other parts of your world.

After the social interaction comes the intellectual level of your relationship. A relationship cannot survive on emotions and hormones alone. You move from the social or group aspect to the conversational. Note that girls tend to need the conversation side of relationships much more than boys. On this level you discover things you have in common. You need more to talk about than surface issues and small talk. Discussing the football game and your ability to burp the alphabet will only carry you so far. Talking about deeper issues becomes important on the intellectual level of relationships.

The last and least important level to reach in a relationship according to the world is the spiritual part. This is where a couple looks at the common ground they share in God, Allah, Buddha, the New Age, Nature, or many other gods. This is the least important step according to the world's view when getting to know someone and allows for tolerance in all areas of spirituality. God is not the only god. Many apply little or no significance to this stage of a relationship.

Hold up your hand again. Your thumb is still number one, the physical attraction in a relationship. But now, turn your hand around so that the little finger is now in the place the thumb previously held. God's point of view is the opposite of the world's. Now number one is the spiritual aspect of a relationship. See the diagram on the next page to illustrate this point.

What If? Freedom Ministries ~ P.O. Box 470252 ~ Tulsa, Oklahoma 74147-0252 ~ 918-249-FREE (3733) ~ www.whatifministires.com

73

Five Levels of Relationships

God's View

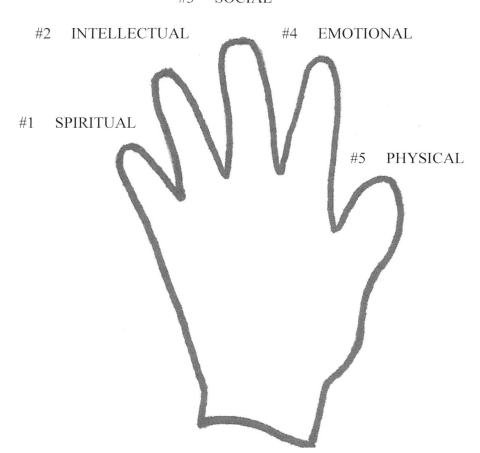

#3   SOCIAL

#2   INTELLECTUAL   #4   EMOTIONAL

#1   SPIRITUAL

#5   PHYSICAL

What If? Freedom Ministries ~ P.O. Box 470252 ~ Tulsa, Oklahoma 74147-0252 ~ 918-249-FREE (3733) ~ www.whatifministires.com

74

God's priority is for you to be a mighty man of honor, a man of high moral character. The Bible was written to give you direction for your life and how to relate to others. If the spiritual side of your life is in order, the rest of your life will fall into its proper place. God's instruction book promotes health – physically, emotionally, mentally, and spiritually. The first requirement for healthy relationships is for you to be a healthy young man. You take care of your body by eating well, exercising, and getting enough rest. Emotionally, guard your heart and do not entangle your emotions with those who are not uplifting you. Mentally, you go to school and study to prepare for your future. You have also learned the importance of focusing your mind on the good and right things of life. Spiritually, study God's Word, listen to others who know God and obey His Word, honor your parents, and put God first in your life. God has great plans for you as you prepare for adulthood. With your priorities right, He will keep you on target to be the warrior He made you to be.

As you saw in the last few pages, our culture has warped God's plan for relationships. When you want to begin a relationship with a young lady, the first level in a godly association should focus on the spiritual aspects. Are both your relationships with God focused on the same thing? Do both of you desire for God to be first in your individual lives and in your relationship? Do you pray together? Do you study The Bible together and individually? Can you discuss what God is teaching you and grow closer to God as the relationship grows? A good indication that the relationship is on track is that you are becoming closer to God and your family as the relationship continues. Be wary of any that take you away from God and seem to drive a wedge between you and your parents or other godly people in your life. God wants first place in your life. Any relationship that is more important to you than God is an idol.

The second level of God's view of relationships is the intellectual. On this plane you both want to grow intellectually. You discuss things of importance, not just the weather or the latest movie. Men typically do not need to talk as much as women do, but conversation is a valuable part of relationships. Talk about what you enjoy, your goals in life, what God is teaching you, and any number of topics. God gave you a great brain; use it. What better way to get to know a girl than to talk about what matters most to you and to her. You need to know how your future bride thinks – before the honeymoon.

The third level of relationships is in the same position for the world's and God's view. The social level involves interaction with others. Be cautious with whom you associate. Someone has said that if you show me your friends, I will show you your future. Think about that! Surround yourself with people who build you up and support you in your goals and relationship with God. This is especially important if you have a girlfriend. As relationships develop, the important "one" in your life wields enormous influence over you. Embracing the social part of your life also protects you. Having godly people around you shields you from the temptation that arises when a couple is alone battling hormones and whispers from the devil.

Taking a girl on a date should never be a game of conquest. Respect is of the utmost importance on both your parts. Being alone together puts you into situations that allow

What If? Freedom Ministries ~ P.O. Box 470252 ~ Tulsa, Oklahoma 74147-0252 ~ 918-249-FREE (3733) ~ www.whatifministires.com

75

your hormones to take control and you do things you vowed you never would. Do you get off by yourself in a car, watch a movie alone together in a dark room, or do you spend time together with a bunch of friends or family? Create a safe environment for dating. There is safety and a lot of fun in numbers. Enjoy the social aspect of relationships. Before you go out, discuss your boundaries with your date (a good topic for the intellectual level of the relationship) so you can support each other in your determination to follow God's plan for your lives. Guard your future and her future.

Once the first three levels are in sync, step back and take some time to evaluate the relationship. This is not a casual evaluation and should preferably occur in your later teens or 20's. Enjoy all your friends as you are becoming who God intended you to be. Pairing off early in your teens limits what you experience and how you see your future. Remember, you live in a microwave mentality society where speed is all important. In God's world, patience is a virtue. Allow your relationship to develop according to God's timetable. He never rushes. God is never late. He is also rarely early. If the young lady is to be your future wife, God will work out the details. If she is not, you do not want to become entangled with her for momentary pleasure.

Many believe that going to sleep to your emotions and hormones is the best way to handle the teen years. When God made Eve from Adam's rib, He put him to sleep. What if Adam slept while Eve was created to keep his hormones and emotions in check? You do not want to trifle with girls' affections just to satisfy the craving you have from hormones and emotions going off in your body. Try asking God to put you asleep to this turmoil. A good soldier cannot fight every battle that comes along. He knows when to rest and ignore skirmishes that distract him from his focus and the real purpose of his mission. Give your heart to your parents or other trusted adult for safekeeping for a time. While they cover you with their protection and prayer, you are free to focus on becoming the man of God that He wants you to be. Ask the Holy Spirit to help you with this challenge and to awaken you in God's perfect timing. You will not have to shop around and go looking for your bride. God will bring her into your life at the ideal time and place. Why would you want to settle for second best when God has the BEST picked out for you? In this way, you will guard your heart and body from relationships that never should have been. You will indeed be a one-woman man who saved all of his heart for his wife.

These next two paragraphs are for future reference but helpful to plant ideas for you as you consider marriage. If you feel certain that you have met God's choice for you and the first three levels of God's desire in relationships have been completed, then go to your parents and/or your spiritual leaders by yourself. Share your thoughts with them and how you believe you have progressed through the three steps. Ask for their advice. Pray together and seek God's direction. If your parents and spiritual leaders are in agreement that this is of the Lord, go to the girl's father and discuss your desires with him. This part of the process can protect you in many ways. God's blessing is on a relationship that He has ordained. The significant adults in your lives are involved and watching out for your safety and integrity. You will have the blessing of the girl's father. What a wonderful way to begin. At this point, you and she are ready for a special relationship. You may

What If? Freedom Ministries ~ P.O. Box 470252 ~ Tulsa, Oklahoma 74147-0252 ~ 918-249-FREE (3733) ~ www.whatifministires.com

76

call it courting or betrothing. The name is not important. What is important is that God is in the center of your decision, not hormones, emotions, peer pressure, or bragging rights.

Now you are ready for the next level, the emotional aspect. This does NOT mean that now you can allow your emotions to take control. But the two of you share deeper thoughts and godly desires. You begin a bonding process as you prepare for marriage. The emotions are not based so much on hormones as they are on a deep commitment and respect for each other and God. You begin to share your intimate thoughts about life and how God is shaping your future together. The emotions are controlled by your individual and joint commitments to God and by knowing that God is in charge of your relationship.

Step five in God's order is the physical aspect. Mentally and physically, save this level for after you are married. If you have been having thoughts about her body and what it would be like to be in bed with her, you have violated her honor and yours. Stay mentally pure. When you are tempted by improper thoughts, stop and pray for your future bride. Replace those wrong thoughts. Ask God to keep both of you pure-in-heart in every respect. Have some favorite scriptures memorized to quote when temptation arrives. Once you are married, your body belongs to your wife and her body belongs to you. It is well worth the wait. Think of the delight and contentment you will enjoy on your wedding night knowing that you have saved yourself entirely – body, soul, and spirit – for your one woman.

In our culture it is all too common to violate God's standards for relationships. The widely accepted dating practices promote the world's view of relationships at every turn. Sex before marriage is rarely condemned. If you plan to remain a virgin until marriage, many will make fun of you. Be prepared to stand firm. People will question your manhood and taunt you to go along with the crowd. Listen, it takes more courage to take a stand for righteousness, to save yourself for marriage, than it does to violate a young lady no matter how willing she may be. There are plenty of girls who are saving themselves for their Mighty Warrior. You just need to wait for God to bring her into your life.

You cannot take a girl's virginity without creating physical and emotional scars that may last a lifetime. For a moment of pleasure, you rob each other of the special gift reserved for your wife and her husband. Even though sexually active teens may look happy on the outside, depression and isolation grow out of inappropriate activities. Promiscuous sexual activity also opens you up to the possibility of pregnancy and sexually transmitted diseases. Is it worth the risk? There are over 20 STDs, and none of them can be cured. Some lead to death. There is not one orgasm in this world that is worth dying for. Safe sex is NOT!

What if you have already violated God's plan for relationships? If you have crossed the line sexually, THERE IS STILL HOPE. God is the God of the second chance. Proverbs 24:16 (NIV) says, "For though a righteous man falls seven times, he rises again...." When you fail, pick yourself up, brush off your pants, and try again. Abba Father has

What If? Freedom Ministries ~ P.O. Box 470252 ~ Tulsa, Oklahoma 74147-0252 ~ 918-249-FREE (3733) ~ www.whatifministires.com

77

only your best interests at heart. His rules are meant for your protection, not to prevent you from having fun. He is full of mercy and grace. You can never sin too much for God not to forgive you. You may have fathered a child, or you may have violated many girls in your mind. Wherever you stand right now in regards to sexual purity, God is ready to stand with you. Your parents and godly leaders are ready to stand with you. Draw a line in the sand and decide today not to cross that boundary. The enemy would have you believe that you are too far gone, you have fallen and can't get up. Satan will whisper in your ear that God has no use for you, no forgiveness. The devil is the master of lies. His goal is to destroy you. Believe Truth!

God's desire is to restore you to fullness and health in every part of your life. All you have to do is ask Him to forgive you and repent of your behavior. Repent means to change. God will help you change your behavior. The path will be hard. Once you have given territory to the enemy, it is harder to take it back. But harder does not mean impossible. Nothing is impossible with God. Make the decision to become a secondary virgin. That is someone who has crossed the line sexually but has committed to remain pure from now until marriage. Go to a few godly, trustworthy friends and ask them to help you in this new life style. Be open and honest. Pray together, and seek God's direction continually. You are important to God. He is watching you and saying, "That's My boy." He does not condemn you. Just like the story of the Prodigal Son, your heavenly Father is waiting for you. Give Him a chance to show Himself strong in you.

Study the following scriptures and write what God reveals to you.

Deuteronomy 22:20-30

_____

_____

Proverbs 6:25-27

_____

_____

1Timothy 5:1-6

_____

_____

What If? Freedom Ministries ~ P.O. Box 470252 ~ Tulsa, Oklahoma 74147-0252 ~ 918-249-FREE (3733) ~ www.whatifministires.com

78

2 Peter 1:2-7

_____

_____

Memory verse – Romans 12:1-2 (NIV)

Therefore, I urge you, brothers, in view of God's mercy, to offer your bodies as living sacrifices, holy and pleasing to God – this is your spiritual act of worship. Do not conform any longer to the pattern of this world, but be transformed by the renewing of your mind. Then you will be able to test and approve what God's will is – his good, pleasing and perfect will.

Thinking Points

King David looked at Bathsheba, thought about how beautiful she was, and finally acted on his thoughts. What lessons can you learn from King David? (2 Samuel 11 & 12:1-25)

_____

_____

_____

The story of the Prodigal Son is found in Luke 15:11-24. Can you relate to this story? How?

_____

_____

_____

What If? Freedom Ministries ~ P.O. Box 470252 ~ Tulsa, Oklahoma 74147-0252 ~ 918-249-FREE (3733) ~ www.whatifministires.com

79

Do girls have to deserve honor for you to treat them as a valuable vessel? List three ways you can honor the girls in your life.

_____

_____

_____

Ask God to show you how far is too far when you are with a girl. Write what He speaks to you.

_____

_____

_____

What changes in your attitudes and actions toward girls do you need to make to be more like the man of God that He wants you to be?

_____

_____

_____

Write your boundaries regarding the girls in your life. Share these with your mentor and/or accountability partner.

_____

_____

_____

What If?
God understands your teenage emotions and turmoil but still believes in you and your ability to be a Mighty Warrior.

What If? Freedom Ministries ~ P.O. Box 470252 ~ Tulsa, Oklahoma 74147-0252 ~ 918-249-FREE (3733) ~ www.whatifministires.com

Chapter 8
Take the Offensive

Have you heard the phrase, "The best defense is a good offense"? It's time to take action, to plan your offensive strategy. Now is the time to be the Mighty Warrior, the man God has called you to be. In every war you must have a battle plan to coordinate your line of attack against the enemy. Without a plan in place, your tactics are hit and miss. To fight the best fight, develop a strategy to cut off the enemy before he pulls a sneak attack on you.

BOUNDARIES

A good place to start is to set boundaries. The first thing a soldier does when he captures territory is to establish a perimeter of the area. He secures the borders. As a man of honor, it is important that you secure the borders of your territory. Think of boundaries as a fence around your "house," the temple of the Holy Spirit. Your physical house has a property line that indicates the exact amount of territory you own. Even without a fence, most people respect the border of your yard. Likewise, set up boundaries around your mind, body, and heart. When appropriate, let others know what your boundaries are. Make sure that you know your boundaries and do not violate them. They are for your protection. Without boundaries, your life is out of control; and you open yourself up to attacks from the enemy. Write down your boundaries to keep them in front of you as a reminder. They determine how you will live your life. When you were a child, your family set boundaries for you. The older you are the more boundaries you set for yourself.

You already have boundaries but may not realize it. For example, you have certain standards regarding the music you listen to, the TV programs and movies you watch, and friends you have. The question is, "Are your standards God's standards?" What are your boundaries on the internet? Many young men think they can look at pornography a little at a time and have no negative results. That is a dangerous boundary. Each time you look, your border is compromised. Do you have godly boundaries that you enforce when you are with a girl? Where do you look? What do you talk about? What do you do? It is critical to set boundaries in advance and obey them. For example, you might never allow yourself to be alone with the opposite sex to avoid temptation. Consider setting a boundary that all dates will be in a public place. You could decide in your heart never to talk about girls with the guys. Many girls' reputations have been damaged by locker room talk. Think about the boundaries you need to set in your life. Ask a friend to hold you accountable to follow your own rules.

Your mind is programmable, and you are the only one that controls the programming. The world tries to convince you to eat and drink certain products, buy their brand of clothes, listen to their music, and watch television and movies based on their standard, not God's. The more you watch or listen to propaganda, the more deeply it affects you. That is why those at war use the internet and other media to bombard the world with their

What If? Freedom Ministries ~ P.O. Box 470252 ~ Tulsa, Oklahoma 74147-0252 ~ 918-249-FREE (3733) ~ www.whatifministires.com

81

perspective. If you only see or hear the enemy's side of the story, your resolve is damaged. You, the soldier, are weakened.

Let's review muscle memory. Remember how Phil trained his muscles to do the iron cross on the rings in gymnastics? His training made grooves in his mind and muscles to be able to do the skill automatically. A similar phenomenon occurs in your mind. The more you see or hear something, the greater impact it has upon you. It becomes imbedded in your thoughts and begins making a little groove in your brain. With each repetition, the groove becomes deeper. Every time you allow your imagination to slip into inappropriate thoughts, pornography, or sexual fantasies, you create a groove in your brain. The groove may start out very small. You look at a girl and undress her in your mind. You do not have to act on the thought for the groove to begin. Every time you go there again, the path deepens. Little by little the thoughts take control of your mind. That is the danger of dabbling in sinful activities. The thoughts quickly multiply and before you know it, you are consumed with sexual feelings.

You are an honorable young man. Fight the dark urges that enter your brain. Even godly men can succumb to the enemy's tactics if boundaries are not enforced. Surfing the internet unfiltered, watching a sexually enticing advertisement on TV, or watching an R or X-rated movie deepens those grooves in your brain. Experimenting with pornography, fondling a girl, or participating in other sexual activities as a "one-time" adventure are invitations to sinful activities. Satan's offense is to convince you that "one time" will not matter. Surely, you are strong enough to resist. The truth is that each time you fall for that lie it becomes an easier and more automatic response in your mind. The enemy arouses feelings and thoughts to entice you to return again and again.

What are you to do? What is your offensive strategy? Set boundaries. You know what arouses those feelings within you. These are called triggers. Learn to recognize the triggers. It may be certain days of the week; particular times of the day; certain places (home, school, car); specific people; emotional times when you are confident, sad, happy, tired, depressed, rejected, or angry. To help you learn to recognize your specific triggers, track them for a week. Make a chart and record what you were feeling or thinking just before your mind wandered into wrong thinking. At the end of the week, review the information and write down your personal triggers. Then find ways to replace those triggers with positive activities so you do not violate your boundaries for integrity. It is important to understand that just trying to avoid them does not work. The more you try to avoid, the more you think about it, and the more likely you are to succumb to the temptation. Replace the triggers with exercise, scripture, a song, a phone call to a friend – anything that takes your mind off the trigger and its response. Do not stay alone with your triggers. A soldier fights better within his unit. Get with a friend and confide in each other. Notice the word "confide." That means what you share together goes no further than the two of you. Never spread information told you in private to anyone else. Let your reputation state that you can keep your mouth shut. God did not intend for you to be alone in this life. Choose your friends wisely. Make sure they support you and not tear you down. And you be that same kind of friend.

What If? Freedom Ministries ~ P.O. Box 470252 ~ Tulsa, Oklahoma 74147-0252 ~ 918-249-FREE (3733) ~ www.whatifministires.com

82

BOUNCE YOUR EYES

Another offensive tactic is to learn to bounce your eyes. If you see something that exceeds your boundaries, look away immediately. Follow the two-second rule. Do not allow yourself to dwell on the image for even a couple seconds. Bounce your eyes. The longer you look, the more deeply imbedded the image becomes in your mind (muscle memory). Do not allow the grooves to deepen. When you see a sexually alluring commercial begin on TV, bounce your eyes, change the channel, or walk away. When you are at the mall and see a display window full of lingerie, bounce your eyes. When you see a girl with too much skin exposed, bounce your eyes. There is strength in numbers, so enlist some of your buddies to practice bouncing eyes along with you. Remember, men are visually stimulated, so it is extremely important that you learn and apply bouncing your eyes. Every time you bounce your eyes and thoughts away from a sexually tempting scene, your positive memory groove becomes deeper and more powerful. At first, you may have to think about the action to bounce your eyes before you actually look away. Do not give up. Continue to practice. It will become an automatic response.

SWORD OF THE SPIRIT

The sword is an offensive and defensive weapon. The Bible is called the Sword of the Spirit. One of the most valuable weapons to implement your strategy is The Word of God. You cannot overemphasize the value of scripture as an offensive tool. Satan's primary target in your battle is your mind. If he can conquer your thought processes, he will defeat you. With your mind filled with scripture, the enemy does not stand a chance. Your responsibility is to fill your mind with The Word so that quoting scripture becomes another automatic response. The Sword also refers to your own words. Proverbs 18:21 says you hold the power of life and death in your tongue. Your words have great power for good or evil. Focus on the good. What you store in your mind goes to your heart. Out of your heart come the words you speak. Talking about yourself and others with God's Truth provokes the devil and defeats his strategy against you. Use your Sword with power.

The point of training is to prepare the soldier to react automatically in the heat of battle the way he was trained. If you train your mind and body continually to follow The Word of God, you will react properly in the midst of battle. Memorize scriptures that give you added strength when attacked. The more you lean on the Holy Spirit to fight with you and for you, the easier the battle becomes. Learn the Truth to fight against the lies of Satan. Write out Bible verses on 3x5 cards to have with you at all times. Put them on your computer or in your cell phone. Most importantly, store them in your brain so you have the ammunition to replace wrong thoughts with Truth.

TIME WITH GOD

Studying The Bible complements another offensive strategy, spending time with God. Getting to know God and understanding His character gives you a great advantage over

What If? Freedom Ministries ~ P.O. Box 470252 ~ Tulsa, Oklahoma 74147-0252 ~ 918-249-FREE (3733) ~ www.whatifministires.com

83

the enemy. The more you experience God and His love in your life, the deeper you trust Him. As you allow your Father to direct your steps, He keeps you under the shadow of His wing, and you are less vulnerable to the devil. If you see God as a mean disciplinarian, critical of everything you do, you cannot run to Him for protection when in danger. Spending time with Him shows you Who He really is. God is a good God who has only the best in store for you.

HONESTY

Honesty is an amazing weapon against the devil. Many try to hide their true feelings and actions from God. Think about that. God knows everything. He sees all that you do and understands what is going on inside you better than you do. Nothing surprises Him. You do not have to be afraid to tell God what you really think. You can even yell at God or tell Him you are angry with Him. He is big enough to handle that. He knows how you feel anyway. Why not get it out in the open? Honesty with God frees you to experience a real closeness with Him.

That paves the way to be open and honest in other relationships. A transparent person is a victorious soldier. Satan flourishes when you lie and try to hide sinful behavior. One of his powerful strategies is to tempt you to do something and then condemn you for doing it. He is masterful at making you feel guilty about the very thing he coerced you to do. The more guilt and shame he can heap on you, the more power he has over you. If you lie or try to hide your sin, you are only compounding the problem. Take the offensive. Everyone makes mistakes. It may be embarrassing to admit your mistakes, and you may have consequences to pay. But the sooner you are honest about your sin and confess it, the sooner you can get back into the war as a Mighty Warrior. It takes a very courageous man to admit he was wrong and to ask for forgiveness. The rewards are amazing. Most people are quite forgiving. God always forgives when you repent. The relief you experience is miraculous. Your loving Father lifts the weight from your shoulders and joins you in the battle against your enemy. That is why the devil works to keep you in darkness and denial. Hiding your failures in your war for righteousness allows him to torment you and trick you into additional sinful behavior. The moment you recognize a failure, take the offensive by being open and honest.

OBEDIENCE

Obedience is an important part of offensive strategies. During military training, soldiers are taught instant obedience. They learn not to question an order but to follow the leader's direction without fail. This may sound foreign to you. A part of each person's nature hates to do what he is told. The flesh says I'll do it my way. I know better than those who have gone before me. That kind of thinking is rebellious and dangerous. Rules, laws, and orders are not given to provoke you to rebel. They are put in place to help you avoid mistakes and to protect you from your enemies. For example, when you were a boy, you were told not to touch the hot stove. Were your parents trying to keep you from enjoying a great pleasure? Of course not. They knew that the stove could burn you, cause you pain. As a teenager, you may be learning to drive. What would happen if

What If? Freedom Ministries ~ P.O. Box 470252 ~ Tulsa, Oklahoma 74147-0252 ~ 918-249-FREE (3733) ~ www.whatifministires.com

84

there were no traffic laws? The streets and highways would be chaos. Traffic laws were made for motorists' protection. Rules for purity may seem ridiculous to you. It is common to feel invincible during your teens. You can handle any situation that may arise, right? If that were the case, why are STDs, teen pregnancy, depression, isolation, and suicide such serious issues? The enemy would have you believe that your parents and God are hiding the best things in life from you. The enemy is a liar. Keeping an honorable heart, mind, and body protects you from emotional trauma and physical ailments. Moral character is for your protection. Obedience to God's Word and your parents' rules shields you from the enemy's plan for your life – destruction and misery.

Instant obedience is a soldier's friend. If you are on the battlefield and your commander shouts, "Hit the dirt!" your obedience may save your life. A soldier who questions the wisdom of his leader puts his life and the others in his unit in jeopardy. When you are on the front lines of this war, your compliance is critical. As you train yourself to obey, take one step at a time. Obey in the little things of life to develop a pattern of obedience. Following parents' guidelines regarding where you go and with whom you associate protects you from Satan's traps to lure you into temptation. Obeying curfew guards you and your friends. Your conscience often warns you of danger. If you have an uneasy feeling about watching a certain movie, leave the theater. If you are driving a girl to a secluded spot "to talk," listen to that small voice and obey it instantly. Drive away. Plan activities that include like-minded people who will encourage you to enforce your boundaries. Obey the rules of God's code of conduct for warriors. This means that you plan your strategy for honor so that you do not allow yourself to be in a compromising situation where it is easy for your flesh or hormones to take control. Obeying before you put yourself in danger is always better than suffering consequences after the fact.

Obedience becomes easy when you know your commander well and realize that he is in the position of leadership because he has experienced battle ahead of you; he is aware of the dangers and knows the best way to fight the enemy. A good leader generates loyalty by enforcing the rules fairly and challenging his soldiers to be the best that they can be. If he is firm yet fair, his troops will follow him wherever he leads. They fear him in a healthy way because he holds great power over them. But they trust him with their very lives because they know and respect him. They understand he will push them to their limits, guide them where they need to go, and stay with them throughout the battle.

Your Commander-in-Chief is like that. An amazing offense begins with the fear of the Lord. The Bible states that the fear of the Lord is the beginning of wisdom. (Proverbs 1:7) Does that mean you should be afraid of God? Absolutely not. To fear the Lord means to be in awe of Him, to respect Him. Rather than be afraid of God's punishment, stand in awe of His great love for you. Consider how wonderful it is that He cares enough for your well being that He provides rules and direction for every aspect of your life. The dietary laws of the Old Testament protected the Israelites before scientists discovered bacteria. Rules for sexual purity shield you from disease and emotional distress. Try adjusting your perspective to see God as your protector, your teacher, your counselor, your leader. He is everything you need Him to be. Stand in awe of Him.

What If? Freedom Ministries ~ P.O. Box 470252 ~ Tulsa, Oklahoma 74147-0252 ~ 918-249-FREE (3733) ~ www.whatifministires.com

85

FORGIVENESS

You may not consider forgiveness to be an offensive weapon, but it is. Unforgiveness on your part stands between you and God. That ties God's hands in His efforts to lead you. It is a hindrance to hearing God's voice and maintaining that close, personal friendship with your Father. You must practice forgiveness if you are to fight effectively. You see, forgiving benefits you much more than the person you forgive. If you do not forgive, anger, bitterness, hatred, and other emotions fester inside you rendering you helpless. Holding on to negative emotions makes you miserable. Ironically, often the person you refuse to forgive has no idea how you feel and goes happily on with life oblivious to your pain.

Focus on God's love and His forgiveness toward you. Eventually that love will transfer to those who have hurt you. It is a process in which time helps to heal the wounds. Choose not to be offended. Refuse to rehearse the offenses in your mind. Each time you do that it is as if you are picking open a scab in your heart. What happens if you remove a scab on your knee every day? The wound will never heal completely, and an ugly scar can develop. It is the same with emotional wounds. Allow the healing balm of God's love to heal the wounds as you keep your mind's eye focused on Jesus and what great things He has done for you.

It is important to understand that forgiving a person does not equate to condoning the behavior. Forgiveness is an act of your will. But it is appropriate to enforce boundaries against wrong behavior even though you have forgiven the person. It is a mistake to equate forgiveness with allowing the offender to continue hurting you through words and actions. That is wrong thinking. Renew your mind to forgive people quickly but to establish boundaries for your protection physically, mentally, emotionally, and spiritually when needed. You can then walk in freedom.

Forgiveness is a choice that brings peace to you and empowers you to live life in freedom. Choose not to be offended or angry even when you feel you have every right not to forgive. In this world, you cannot avoid all evil or mean people. You will be hurt and offended. You can then follow Satan's plan to remain bitter and miss out on God's blessings or choose to forgive, even when forgiveness is undeserved. That is the key to entering God's rest. Do you want to be forgiven for mistakes you make? Do you deserve to be forgiven? No, none of us deserves forgiveness. We deserve to go to hell. But Jesus took all our sins on Himself when He died on the cross. Since He is perfect and never sinned, Jesus deserves God's love. Because He is your substitute, you too can receive God's love and forgiveness. That is His gift to you as well as your enemies. Follow Jesus' example and offer forgiveness and mercy liberally.

Consider this. After being beaten beyond recognition and nailed on the cross to die, how did Jesus respond? He could have said, "Hey, Dad, zap 'em! I've changed my mind. Get me out of here." But He didn't. While hanging naked on the cross and hearing the soldiers and crowd mock, criticize, ridicule, and disrespect Him, one of His last comments was, "Father, forgive them. They don't know what they are doing." Asking

What If? Freedom Ministries ~ P.O. Box 470252 ~ Tulsa, Oklahoma 74147-0252 ~ 918-249-FREE (3733) ~ www.whatifministires.com

86

God to help you see others through His eyes and with His perspective provides a powerful weapon for your offensive arsenal.

The Bible says to love – everyone. In fact, Jesus said to love your enemies and to pray for those who persecute you. Do you ever feel persecuted? Do you consider your parents or any other adults as enemies? What about rivals at school or in your neighborhood? It is easy to be nice to and love those who are nice to you. Anyone can do that. But a Mighty Warrior must go the extra mile and love even his enemies. What if you would choose to pray for those you think are your enemies? Try it; you might like it. This could be life changing. Remember the real enemy is Satan, the deceiver and your accuser. If you have anger, funnel it toward your true adversary.

PRAISE, WORSHIP, JOY, AND PRAYER

The absolute most powerful tools at your disposal are praise, worship, joy, and prayer. This war is in the spirit world. When you pray and worship, you release missiles of mass destruction into the atmosphere all around you. They are pre-emptive strikes against Satan. In Old Testament wars, the priests went before the warriors to pave the way with prayer and praise before each battle. This placed their focus on Jehovah and invited God to fight with them and for them. Whenever God joins you in battle, you win.

The story of King Jehoshaphat in 2 Chronicles 20:15-25 (NIV) gives an interesting perspective to God's strategy. The king had been informed that a great army had assembled to fight against Judah. The first response as the people gathered together was to seek help from the Lord. After prayer, the Spirit of the Lord spoke to the people. "Do not be afraid or discouraged because of this vast army. For the battle is not yours, but God's.... You will not have to fight this battle. Take up your position; stand firm and see the deliverance the Lord will give you.... Jehoshaphat bowed with his face to the ground, and all the people of Judah and Jerusalem fell down in worship before the Lord." Notice that the first thing the people did was pray. Then they waited for God's answer with a prayerful and expectant attitude. When they heard from heaven, they took their position and stood still before God. Here is the key; their position was one of worship. The next morning they assembled for battle. The king "appointed those who should sing to the Lord, and who should praise the beauty of holiness, as they went out **before** the army and were saying: Praise the Lord, for His mercy endures forever." The people of Judah prayed, waited, worshipped, and praised. Their reward was that the enemy was self-slaughtered, and it took three days to gather the spoils of war because there was so much.

Your position for battle begins bowed before your Father God in worship and submission to Him. Prayer and praise fend off the enemy's attacks. When you are tempted to yell at your parents, stop and say a silent prayer or begin to praise the Lord. You have just defeated the devil. If you are tortured by pornographic thoughts, shout that the joy of the Lord is your strength. Develop the habit to praise and worship at the beginning of the battle. Use that as your first offensive weapon of choice, not as an after thought. Pray without ceasing; just talk to God like He is your best Friend. He is ready at a moment's

What If? Freedom Ministries ~ P.O. Box 470252 ~ Tulsa, Oklahoma 74147-0252 ~ 918-249-FREE (3733) ~ www.whatifministires.com

87

notice to provide reinforcements. Your Command-in-Chief is faithful and trustworthy. Follow Him. Allow Him to lead you in every part of this war. The same God who fought for Judah is available to you, Mighty Warrior. Prayer, praise, joy, and worship still work today.

Write what God shows you about the following scriptures.

Nehemiah 8:10

_____

_____

Proverbs 2:1-5

_____

_____

Proverbs 4:20-27

_____

_____

Matthew 6:14-15

_____

_____

Ephesians 4:17-19

_____

_____

What If? Freedom Ministries ~ P.O. Box 470252 ~ Tulsa, Oklahoma 74147-0252 ~ 918-249-FREE (3733) ~ www.whatifministires.com

88

1 Thessalonians 5:15-18

_____

_____

2 Timothy 2:15

_____

_____

Memory verse – Psalm 56:3-4 (NIV)

When I am afraid, I will trust in you. In God, whose word I praise, in God I trust; I will not be afraid. What can mortal man do to me?

Thinking Points

What is your number one offensive weapon in your war chest? Why?

_____

_____

_____

Give an example of a time when you hid the truth and suffered consequences. How could being open and honest have changed the outcome?

_____

_____

_____

What If? Freedom Ministries ~ P.O. Box 470252 ~ Tulsa, Oklahoma 74147-0252 ~ 918-249-FREE (3733) ~ www.whatifministires.com

89

In what areas of your life is it most difficult for you to obey? What can you do to improve your compliance?

_____

_____

_____

How many times should you forgive someone? Does it change depending on the offense? Justify your answer.

_____

_____

_____

Write in your own words what the fear of the Lord means to you. Do you need to make any adjustments to your attitude toward your Commander-in-Chief? If so, describe them.

_____

_____

_____

Write two or three changes you will make as a result of charting your triggers.

_____

_____

_____

What if?
God chooses to forgive you every time you ask and cannot remember your offense once He has forgiven you.

What If? Freedom Ministries ~ P.O. Box 470252 ~ Tulsa, Oklahoma 74147-0252 ~ 918-249-FREE (3733) ~ www.whatifministires.com

90

Chapter 9
Secure the Perimeter

> Son of man, I have made you a watchman for the house of Israel; so
> hear the word I speak, and give them warning from Me. But if you do
> warn the righteous man not to sin and he does not sin, he will surely
> live because he took warning, and you will have saved yourself.
> Ezekiel 3:17, 21 (NIV)

In the Old Testament, the watchman's job was to warn the town's citizens of impending danger. Cities were fortified by walls that were thick and high so that it was difficult for the enemy to penetrate. Watchmen were stationed atop the wall to watch for any sign of approaching danger. What if the watchman let down his guard? The entire city was placed at risk, and the result would often be loss of life and property. Hopefully, you have established the wall for your city, the boundaries for your life to protect your integrity. In addition to boundaries, you need to place sentries around that perimeter to shout out warnings of incoming trouble. Sound the alarm. Tell someone! When soldiers establish a perimeter around their encampments, sentries are immediately stationed at regular intervals. Without guardians, the enemy can easily infiltrate the camp, your life.

You determine what guardians you create for yourself. What can you put in place around your perimeter to warn you when danger is approaching? It only takes one breech to infiltrate and destroy. Take God's warnings seriously. Maintain constant vigilance. The enemy is watching and waiting for any opportunity to break down your defenses. Never drop your guard. That is a huge order but essential to hold your ground in the battle.

Your primary guardian is the Holy Spirit. God is the Commander-in-Chief, your five-star general. But the generals are rarely down in the trenches with the troops. They stand back to view the entire battleground to have the proper perspective on all that is happening. When Jesus was preparing His disciples for His return to heaven, he told them that it was good that He would leave. Only after Jesus ascended to heaven could the Holy Spirit come to comfort, help, counsel, and teach them all things. The Holy Spirit is with you in the trenches and is your watchman around your perimeter. Sometimes He shouts out warnings and other times He whispers a caution. Train yourself to hear your Guardian. When the devil tempts you to remove one brick from your wall of protection, the Holy Spirit is your watchman. The enemy may whisper, "All guys look at pornography a little. It is part of becoming a man." The voice of your conscience replies, "Even one look plants harmful images in your brain. Turn away." Your watchman is warning you, a righteous man, not to sin. Sin not and live because you took the warning. That uneasy feeling you experience when you are tempted to undress a girl in your mind is the Holy Spirit trying to get your attention. Be sensitive to those feelings, and run from danger.

Train yourself to hear God's voice. Satan disguises himself as an angel of light. He plants thoughts to create doubt, fear, and rebellion in you. You need to be able to

What If? Freedom Ministries ~ P.O. Box 470252 ~ Tulsa, Oklahoma 74147-0252 ~ 918-249-FREE (3733) ~ www.whatifministires.com

91

distinguish between the voice of Satan and the voice of the Holy Spirit. Be certain that God will never encourage you to do anything that is bad for you or contrary to The Bible. Knowing the Word of God is another Guardian for your mind. His Truth defeats the intruder every time. If you question whether or not you should do something (doubt and confusion), stop. Wait for clearance from your Watchman. He is there to shout out warnings of approaching danger. Stop and wait for clear direction and orders from your Commander.

A healthy fear of the Lord is a good thing. Remember the story of Joseph after he was sold into slavery. (Genesis 39) He was an honorable young man who obeyed God in all that he did. Because of that obedience, he became the head of Potiphar's household. The fear of the Lord, a guardian, directed his every-day actions and behavior. When Potiphar's wife tried to seduce him, Joseph could easily have given in to her request and enjoyed the temporary pleasure of lying in bed with her. However, he was so in tune with God that he fled without looking back. He said, "How then can I do this great evil, and sin against God?" (Genesis 39:9 AMP) Even while in prison for that crime he did not commit, he had no regrets about his decision. He trusted God and lived a holy life in prison. That is a man of honor! Fine tune your senses to hear God's still, small voice so that you will flee danger when warned and never look back. You may suffer the pain of obedience. Joseph endured a long prison term for obeying his godly training. However, the pain of obedience far outweighs the pain of regret. Sad is the warrior who had the opportunity to obey with honor and failed because he did not heed the warnings of the Watchman around his perimeter. In your battle you will suffer. Will your pain be the pain of obedience or the pain of regret?

THOUGHTS

The enemy often tries to attack your thoughts. Although your mind is not a visible target, you must guard your thoughts at all cost. You have studied the importance of thoughts previously, but it is worth reviewing your thought-life here. The unseen boundaries are often harder to guard, so you need to pay close attention to them. What can tear down the perimeter around your mind? Remember, men are visually stimulated. What you see exerts a powerful influence over your thoughts. Guard your eyes from evil. Garbage in yields garbage out. What you think about ends up in your heart. What is in your heart comes out your mouth. Guard your thoughts.

MOUTH

Your words are powerful. The saying, "Sticks and stones may break my bones, but words will never hurt me," is not true. Words spoken in anger or without thinking can create an amazing amount of pain. Your words can be a weapon for evil or good. Any good soldier selects powerful weapons that are edifying – words that build up, not tear down. If your words do not build up a person, do not utter one word. Have you ever been betrayed by a friend's words? It can be like a grenade exploding in your face. Your words are a valuable weapon in your arsenal. Pick them wisely, and use those weapons for good. Guard your tongue.

What If? Freedom Ministries ~ P.O. Box 470252 ~ Tulsa, Oklahoma 74147-0252 ~ 918-249-FREE (3733) ~ www.whatifministires.com

92

Honor your parents with your words. You may not agree with your parents' rules, but The Bible commands that you honor their position as parents. You may disagree and discuss alternatives, but use respectful words when talking with your parents and when talking about them. It does not matter how good or bad your parents are, God will honor you when you obey the commandment to respect your mother and father. Guard your actions as well. Storming out of the room when your parents are talking to you, rolling your eyes in response to their comments, and disobeying their direction are all disrespectful. Try honoring your parents and see how they and God respond.

In the war on sexuality you will be tempted to talk about the girls in your life. Guard your mouth at all costs. Guys often discuss girls and their particular "attributes" in the locker room or hallways at school. What you say, whether it is truth or a lie, about a girl will compliment her or damage her reputation. Character assassination is not an acceptable tactic coming from a man of integrity. No matter what you hear or know about a girl, your assignment is to protect her from evil. Speak no evil yourself, and stop others from destroying a girl's life with ill-chosen words.

What is most important is how you talk about yourself. Many battles are lost because the soldier does not believe in himself. Learn to love yourself – in a healthy way, of course. There is a big difference between being selfish and conceited and seeing yourself as a mighty man of God. If you present yourself as a loser, people will treat you like a loser. If you say you are stupid or worthless, you become like your words. Believe what The Word says about you. God made you just the way you are, and what He makes is excellent. Tame your tongue and speak Truth about yourself, Mighty Warrior that you are.

HEART

Guard your heart. A loving attitude toward others and an obedient spirit make a huge difference in your battle. Be careful what you do with your heart. You may want to ask your parents or a trusted, godly adult to help guard your heart during your teens. Protect your heart, but understand there is a delicate balance between giving your heart away to every girl that crosses your path and building walls around your heart to keep everyone out. Life involves risks. War is full of danger. But victory never comes to the warrior that hides behind walls. To win, you must engage the enemy; but fight with wisdom. Balance helps you stay alert to danger while participating in the engagement. Guarding your heart means that you have boundaries to keep out the bad, but your boundaries must allow good to come in. Be aware of that balance.

YOUR GUARDIAN FORCE

In the next chapter you will learn about guardians or support personnel that God has provided for you. Abba Father is your greatest Guardian. He gives you wisdom and places angels around you. The Holy Spirit is always at your side. Do not minimize the value of your parents and family as guardians of your soul. They know you better than most and care about your happiness and future. Your church family offers more

What If? Freedom Ministries ~ P.O. Box 470252 ~ Tulsa, Oklahoma 74147-0252 ~ 918-249-FREE (3733) ~ www.whatifministires.com

93

guardians to complete your circle of protection around you. You can think of these protectors as sentinels around your perimeter whose job it is to keep you safe, secure, and shielded from the enemy. Your Commander-in-Chief has thought of everything you need for war. He put you right where you are with special guardians to help you win.

Study the following verses and write what God speaks to your heart.

Genesis 39:1-23

_____

_____

Psalm 17:3-5

_____

_____

Proverbs 4:23-27

_____

_____

John 14:16-21

_____

_____

Memory verse – Acts 1:8 (NIV)

But you will receive power when the Holy Spirit comes upon you; and you will be my witnesses in Jerusalem, and in all Judea and Samaria, and to the ends of the earth.

What If? Freedom Ministries ~ P.O. Box 470252 ~ Tulsa, Oklahoma 74147-0252 ~ 918-249-FREE (3733) ~ www.whatifministires.com

94

Thinking Points

Describe an issue where you need to guard your words and actions with your parents.

_____

_____

_____

Have you every damaged a girl's reputation by speaking improperly about her? What guardians can you put in place to avoid that happening again?

_____

_____

_____

Describe some ways that you can guard your heart without keeping everyone at arm's length.

_____

_____

_____

What are some warnings that the Holy Spirit has given you? How did you respond? How could you have responded better?

_____

_____

_____

What If? Freedom Ministries ~ P.O. Box 470252 ~ Tulsa, Oklahoma 74147-0252 ~ 918-249-FREE (3733) ~ www.whatifministires.com

95

List three ways you can guard your thoughts and tongue. Write how you put them into practice this week.

_____

_____

_____

What If?
God has given you the Holy Spirit to watch over you and teach you how to guard your thoughts, words, actions, and heart.

What If? Freedom Ministries ~ P.O. Box 470252 ~ Tulsa, Oklahoma 74147-0252 ~ 918-249-FREE (3733) ~ www.whatifministires.com

96

Chapter 10
Support for the Troops

A critical part of any engagement of war is logistical and moral support. Any time a soldier is abandoned to fend for himself, the battle intensifies and his survival rate decreases. Transportation, lodging, and food provided by the support units improve the ability of the soldiers to fight on the front lines and increase the likelihood of victory. Moral support for the troops is equally important. Communication from family and friends; time set aside for R&R (rest and relaxation); and visits by the commander-in-chief, other high ranking officers, and celebrities from home all serve to boost morale. The combination of each area of support equips the warriors to carry out their missions with excellence.

When fighting, troops may have to sleep in tents to stay close to the battle. For a time they may survive on small rations or MREs (meals ready to eat). Every soldier goes into battle prepared to be away from their normal conveniences for a long time. If they never need to use their rations or sleep on the ground, that is great. But they must be prepared for the possibility that their supply lines may be cut. If that happens, the support units scramble to discover ways to meet the needs of the troops on the battlefield. An amazing example of supply line support occurred from June 24, 1948 through May 11, 1949. The Soviet Union cut off West Berlin, Germany from the rest of the world by blocking all railroad and ground access to the city. The people in West Berlin suffered from lack of the most basic necessities. Out of this crisis arose the Berlin Airlift. Many nations joined together and flew into West Berlin with supplies of food, coal, and other provisions for those trapped inside the ring of the communists. The air crews also dropped bags of candy attached to mini parachutes for the children to boost morale. Without the airlift, the people would have died or succumbed to the enemy.

Just as important as providing supplies is maintaining morale. The mental and emotional attitudes of the soldiers affect their ability to fight successfully. They must believe that they are fighting for a good cause and that they can win. Leaders reminding the soldiers why they are fighting and how they will win motivate the troops to perform at their best. Letters, videos, e-mails, phone calls, and packages from home lift up soldiers on the front. Fearing that the folks back home have lost faith in them and the war discourages and demoralizes the troops. The enemy tries desperately to affect public opinion on the home front and to convince those who may be captured that they are alone in the battle; no one cares about them. To isolate a soldier and convince him that no one thinks about him is an effective way to break the will of even the mightiest warrior.

Your enemy is aware that you require logistical and moral support in your battle. Most teens take for granted that they will have shelter, food, and transportation when needed. However, moral support is another issue. You may often feel as if you are alone, the only one with godly standards in the area of sexuality. You need all the moral support you can find to fight the enemy. Satan is a master manipulator and trickster in his war against

What If? Freedom Ministries ~ P.O. Box 470252 ~ Tulsa, Oklahoma 74147-0252 ~ 918-249-FREE (3733) ~ www.whatifministires.com

97

you. Keep your guard up and enlist the support of others in your fight. Remember, you cannot win the war fighting alone. Utilize the support all around you.

PARENTS

One of your greatest supporters is your parents. Even if you do not have a good relationship with them, more often than not, they are cheering for you and your success in life. You studied about improving family relationships in a previous chapter, but now it is time to enlist your parents in the conflict. Actively cultivate a close relationship with your dad. Phil was a phantom father – there physically at times but never emotionally. Over time his relationships with all of his children have been restored through hard work, many conversations, spending time together, and listening. God restores what has been lost or stolen. Give your dad a chance. And don't forget your mom. Her female perspective can enlighten you in many areas, especially when it comes to sexuality. Each parent offers unique insight. You need them, and they need to be involved with you. Support on the home front improves your morale quickly. Those you live with know you best and can help you when no one else can. A pat on the back may be just what you need one day. Another time simply hearing your dad say he is standing with you or is proud of you can make all the difference when you are being tempted. A mother and father who will pray with you and for you are mighty weapons in your arsenal. You are in a spiritual war. The support and prayers of your parents surround you with strength.

Perhaps you think your parents are a bit weird (or a lot weird). That is a common thought among teens. But don't sell your parents short. Consider the story of Hannah in First Samuel chapters 1 and 2. Hannah was a radical, praying mother. She had no children and agonized over that disgrace. Her rival, who did have children, provoked her and made fun of her for years. Despite the ridicule and through her tears, Hannah continued to pray for a child. At one point, the priest Eli accused her of being drunk because she was praying so fervently. Would Hannah's actions have embarrassed you if she had been your mother? Perhaps. But Hannah's perseverance yielded results. God eventually answered her petitions with the birth of Samuel. He became one of the most important prophets in the history of Israel. Hannah's weird behavior and passionate prayers changed the path of the Jewish nation. Mother's and father's prayers are powerful

If you live in a single parent home, your situation is perhaps a greater challenge. Don't be discouraged. Your family is still one of your greatest support groups. Enlist the help of a favorite aunt or uncle, brother or sister, and grandparents. Seek out a godly man who would "adopt" you as his son to fight alongside you. Be creative in ways to make up for weak spots in this area. God will provide exactly who and what you need to complement your arsenal.

FRIENDS

Your church and youth group form another line of defense and support for you. Being involved with both adults and young people who believe in you and agree with your goals and standards for life can sustain you when temptation strikes. If you are not part

What If? Freedom Ministries ~ P.O. Box 470252 ~ Tulsa, Oklahoma 74147-0252 ~ 918-249-FREE (3733) ~ www.whatifministires.com

98

of a good Bible-teaching church and youth group, find one ASAP. They form a hedge of protection around you. Receiving good teaching and direction for life and having other warriors to lift you up when you are down is important. Your buddies in the trenches know you and understand the war you are fighting. They are fighting the same battles. Learn from each other and stick together. The strength-in-numbers mind set works. Many examples from nature emphasize this. When a lion stalks his prey, where does he attack? He watches and waits for a weaker animal that has fallen behind the herd. He does not jump into the center of 20 to 30 strong animals. He separates one from the group and pounces. Satan, like a roaring lion, does the same thing. If he can isolate you from your support group at church, he has a much higher chance of defeating you. Even in your youth group, pick your support group wisely. The enemy loves to infiltrate to divide and conquer, to manipulate and discourage. Make certain that the focus of the group is Jesus Christ and that the goal is to follow and honor Him in all that you do, especially regarding sexual integrity. There is nothing like being part of a vibrant, Christ-centered youth group to support you each and every day.

God made you to be a social person, to relate to and spend time with other people your age. It is good to have friends to support you. However, peer pressure is a huge issue for teenagers. Peer pressure can be positive and negative. Surround yourself with the positive. Not every "friend" will help you follow the right path. It can be extremely difficult to resist the subtle as well as overt tactics of other teens in your life. When with a group, teens and adults will often participate in activities that they would never consider doing if they were alone. Be aware of this very effective tactic of the devil. So-called friends may wear down your defenses over time and trick you into following the crowd. The fear of rejection by peers and the pressure to conform is powerful. Today, many teens consider viewing pornography normal, having sex before marriage a rite of passage, and dressing to attract the opposite sex smart and stylish. Remaining a virgin until marriage has become a disgrace. Will you be a people pleaser or a God pleaser? Pick your friends wisely and set your standards according to God's Word ahead of time. Know what your limits are before you enter a situation where you have to decide what is right. Better yet, do not allow yourself to be in a situation where temptation or hormones rule over your good judgment. Have a good friend who will reinforce your beliefs with you whenever possible. The buddy system works in the military and in your quest for honor.

Peer pressure comes not only from other guys but also from gals in your life. In today's society, girls are often as aggressive as boys, so you need to have ammunition ready to outmaneuver these advances. Hopefully, you are surrounding yourself with godly young men and women who agree with your choice for integrity. However, the bravest and most loyal warrior can fall into a trap set by the enemy. Stay alert to the gradual lowering of your standards. If you hear yourself saying, "It can never happen to me," RUN. Call a friend; talk to your parents; get help immediately. Virtually every Christian leader that has fallen morally in the past few years believed that they could never do what they did. The subtle peer pressure from today's culture and the lack of accountability are fertile soil for the enemy. Pick your friends wisely and set your standards according to God's Word ahead of time.

What If? Freedom Ministries ~ P.O. Box 470252 ~ Tulsa, Oklahoma 74147-0252 ~ 918-249-FREE (3733) ~ www.whatifministires.com

99

MENTOR

Having a good group of friends who encourages you to follow Christ is essential in your efforts to be a man of honor. But do not neglect the value of older and wiser people. A valuable asset in your support arsenal is a mentor. He is an older man you trust and admire who will offer his wisdom gained from experience and His commitment to Jesus without judgment. One of the most important decisions you can make is to ask a godly man to be your mentor. Remember, he doesn't have to be perfect; no one is. But he must love the Lord and give wise, godly counsel; be someone who will listen; confront you when needed; and be open and honest with you. Prayerfully consider whom you should ask to fulfill the role of mentor in your life.

BAND OF BROTHERS

Having an accountability partner is a must to complete your team. Ask a godly friend to cover your back. This comrade in arms will encourage you to make godly choices, be available to support you whenever needed, and be strong enough not to give in when you are tempted. He will confront in love. Your choice should not be taken lightly. This person can make the difference between victory and defeat. When engaged in combat, the soldier wants the strongest, most determined buddy at his side. Together they will not quit, nor will they give in to the deception of the adversary. They hold each other accountable to follow their training regiment and persevere past their normal endurance levels. They do not succumb to cries of "it's too hard." They push past the pain together as a united team. That is the type of young man you need for your accountability partner. If you call him in the evening, he will make time to listen. If you need him in the middle of the night, he doesn't ask you to call him back at a more convenient time. If you need to meet him in person, he is there for you. Whenever you are tempted to violate your boundaries, he is available to hold you accountable to follow your rules of engagement. Your responsibility is to contact your partner whenever you need his help. He is not a mind reader; confide in him. You are the one who knows where and when your attacks are coming. This is a serious commitment, and both of you must understand the life-and-death importance of this relationship.

CIRCLE OF FRIENDS

Although the one-on-one relationship with your accountability partner is important, a support group of other teens is also helpful. This would be a small group of young men that share the same ideals and morals that you do. All of you would agree together to encourage each other to embrace integrity in mind, body, and spirit. Discuss your standards and write them down for future reference as needed. Help each other stick to them. There is strength in numbers. You are not the only one who wants to live a life of honor. Share your struggles openly and honestly with each other for encouragement. Every young man is tempted in the sexual war. Remember, secrecy is a mighty tool the devil uses. Destroy that tactic by honestly discussing the day-to-day battles you are facing. It may be hard to talk about some battles like wanting to look at pornography,

What If? Freedom Ministries ~ P.O. Box 470252 ~ Tulsa, Oklahoma 74147-0252 ~ 918-249-FREE (3733) ~ www.whatifministires.com

100

masturbating, or failing to control yourself when you were with your girlfriend. But getting your failures out into the light is a huge step in defeating your enemy. Extremely important in this group is confidentiality. It must be a safe place where you know that what you share will be a matter of prayer by the group and not gossip.

At times you must be willing to confront and be confronted. If someone in your group is participating in wrong behavior, go to him in love but firmly address the issue based on scripture. Talk to him alone at first. If he accepts your correction, you have helped him become a better soldier. If he does not, confront again with some of the others in your support group. If he continues to rebel, be prepared to bring in a trusted adult. Your youth pastor could be an excellent choice here. On the other side, you must be willing to be confronted. Someone who truly cares about you will not allow you to continue in dangerous behavior. Confrontation is painful, but the results lead to a stronger, mightier warrior better prepared for the next battle in the war.

GOD

The greatest support you can enlist is that of your heavenly Father. Spend time with God. Reading His Word and listening to His voice will make all the difference in every aspect of your life. Knowing what the Bible teaches helps you make wise choices. Soldiers who spend more time with their leaders understand their tactics better and fight with a more unified purpose. Their morale is high because they know the leader and trust his judgment. Do not neglect the personal support your Commander-in-Chief offers you. A close relationship with God is your best support for purity in your mind and actions

Understanding the importance of logistic and moral support is an important strategy against your enemy. Enlisting the various supports available to you gives you an edge over the devil; your power increases exponentially. Scripture states that one can chase 1,000, but two can put 10,000 to flight. (Deuteronomy 32:30) That is an amazing increase in the odds. Plant that truth deep inside you. Do not allow the enemy to isolate you. The times you need support the most are often the times that young men shun their allies. When you struggle with temptation or a difficult decision, do not withdraw into yourself and stuff your emotions. That is the precise moment you need to call for reinforcements. No matter how difficult it may be to ask for help, **ASK!** Do not allow pride to interfere with your grasp of a lifeline to rescue you from danger. A soldier isolated and alone in battle becomes weak and vulnerable. Choose to stay connected and fight from a united front. God is on your side. God and you make a majority.

Write what the following scriptures mean to you in light of godly support.

1 Samuel 18:1-4

_____

_____

What If? Freedom Ministries ~ P.O. Box 470252 ~ Tulsa, Oklahoma 74147-0252 ~ 918-249-FREE (3733) ~ www.whatifministires.ccm

101

Proverbs 15:31-32

_____

_____

John 12:42-43

_____

_____

1 Corinthians 4:15-17

_____

_____

1 Thessalonians 5:11

_____

_____

Titus 2:1-8

_____

_____

Memory verse – Leviticus 26:8 (NIV)

Five of you will chase a hundred, and a hundred of you will chase ten thousand; and your enemies will fall by the sword before you.

What If? Freedom Ministries ~ P.O. Box 470252 ~ Tulsa, Oklahoma 74147-0252 ~ 918-249-FREE (3733) ~ www.whatifministires.com

102

Thinking Points

What support tools are you already using? What tools will you add to your arsenal of support? How will you use them?

_____

_____

_____

Are you a people pleaser or a God pleaser? Give three examples that explain your answer.

_____

_____

_____

Do you belong to a small group where you feel safe to discuss your struggles and failures? Are you open and honest in this group? If you do not have a safe group, what can you do to organize one?

_____

_____

_____

What qualities are you looking for in a mentor? Who do you think would be a good mentor for you? Will you pray and then ask him to be your mentor? Set a date to meet.

_____

_____

_____

What If? Freedom Ministries ~ P.O. Box 470252 ~ Tulsa, Oklahoma 74147-0252 ~ 918-249-FREE (3733) ~ www.whatifministires.com

103

What qualities are you looking for in an accountability partner? Do you have someone in mind? Set a date to discuss this with him.

_____

_____

.

_____

What If?
God smiles when He sees you making wise choices in relationships.

What If? Freedom Ministries ~ P.O. Box 470252 ~ Tulsa, Oklahoma 74147-0252 ~ 918-249-FREE (3733) ~ www.whatifministires.com

Chapter 11
The Warrior's Armor

Put on the full armor of God, so that you can take your stand against
the devil's schemes. For our struggle is not against flesh and blood,
but against the rulers, against the authorities, against the powers of
this dark world and against the spiritual forces of evil in the heavenly
realms. Therefore put on the full armor of God, so that when the day
of evil comes, you may be able to stand your ground, and after you
have done everything, to stand. Stand firm then, with the belt of truth
buckled around your waist, with the breastplate of righteousness in place,
and with your feet fitted with the readiness that comes from the gospel
of peace. In addition to all this, take up the shield of faith, with which
you can extinguish all the flaming arrows of the evil one. Take the
helmet of salvation and the sword of the Spirit, which is the word of God.
And pray in the Spirit on all occasions with all kinds of prayers and
requests. With this in mind, be alert and always keep on praying for all
the saints.
Ephesians 6:11-18 (NIV)

Every soldier wears protective gear. In biblical times warriors had heavy, full-body
armor to protect their vulnerable organs during encounters with swords and spears. The
modern army uses vehicles with high-tech armor, and soldiers wear Kevlar helmets and
vests for protection. At times, gas masks may be required to survive chemical warfare.
The armor may look different at various times in history, but armor remains a vital part of
the soldiers' equipment. Likewise, wearing your spiritual armor is critical for your
survival.

Even though you are fighting against unseen foes, the battle is an intense one and
sometimes more deceptive because you cannot see the enemy with your physical eyes.
The enemy is there, nonetheless. God designed armor specifically for you. Learn to put
it on every day. These weapons are available because you are a child of God; you have a
relationship with your Commander-in-Chief. Without Him, you are nothing. Having that
relationship with God, walking in His presence daily is the beginning of putting on your
armor.

When David was preparing to fight Goliath, no one believed he could do the job. He was
young. He was small. He had no military training. His brothers mocked him. King
Saul, who approved David's request to meet Goliath, offered his armor to the youth. Saul
wanted David to fight man's way, burdened with heavy weapons and armor that did not
fit. David's trust was in the Lord because he had developed a personal relationship with
Him while in the fields working as a shepherd. He wore God's armor and shouted to
Goliath, "I come to you in the name of the Lord!" With God and his sling shot, David
killed one of the mightiest enemies of the Jewish nation when every other soldier in the

What If? Freedom Ministries ~ P.O. Box 470252 ~ Tulsa, Oklahoma 74147-0252 ~ 918-249-FREE (3733) ~ www.whatifministires.ccm

105

camp was shaking in his boots, frozen and afraid to attack the giant. God's armor still works today when you fight the giants in this war.

For your armor to work at its best, you must be fully surrendered to God. On the battlefield, soldiers need to submit to the leaders and unite as one machine to gain victory. An army unit that is divided in its loyalties will fall. A soldier that is functioning against his training and leaders puts himself and his unit in jeopardy. Your leader is Jesus Christ. You must be united with Him in total submission to His direction and marching orders if you expect victory. Let's take a closer look at your amazing armor.

In Ephesians 6, Paul compares the believers' weapons of warfare to Roman armor. You, too, need to understand the uses of the various pieces of armor so you can apply your spiritual weapons to your greatest advantage. Paul lists seven pieces of armor. As you study the similarity of the physical armor to your spiritual protection, imagine how each piece that God has given you will help you succeed in your battle.

THE BELT OF TRUTH

Of all the pieces of armor, why would Paul mention the belt of Truth first? It was intentional. Although the belt was common and rather ugly, it was an essential part of the Roman soldier's military hardware. Like a belt holds up your pants, this belt held his armor together. If you try to march or fight without a belt on, you can easily become entangled in your pants, trip, and fall victim to your enemy. It was the same for the Roman soldier. His belt held his shield, sword, and daggers. Without it, he would be clumsy and constantly trying to keep everything together. A warrior must be able to move easily and access his weapons quickly if he is to fight effectively. His belt makes that possible.

You cannot fight without your belt of Truth. Since the devil is the master of lies, Truth is a most essential piece of your armor. Without Truth, you will be deceived by the tricks of your adversary. In the battle for your mind, you must believe the Truth about yourself and your authority in Christ. The devil would have you think that you cannot fight and win this war. **The Truth is** that you can do all things through Christ who strengthens you. (Philippians 4:13) The enemy tries to confuse you and make you afraid. **The Truth is** God has not given you a spirit of fear but of power and of love and of a sound mind. (2 Timothy 1:7) You must study Truth and apply it to your life every day. You cannot be a Mighty Warrior without the Truth, the Word of God, at the center of your life.

When you put on your belt of Truth, all your preparation comes together. That means you must spend time reading and studying The Bible. Think about The Word; pray about it. Never let it go out of your mind. The Truth must become so much a part of you that it becomes automatic to think and speak what you have studied in The Bible. With your mind saturated with God's Truth, you have the mind of Christ, think clearly, and react

What If? Freedom Ministries ~ P.O. Box 470252 ~ Tulsa, Oklahoma 74147-0252 ~ 918-249-FREE (3733) ~ www.whatifministires.com

106

properly. You become the Truth – the righteousness of Christ. All the other parts of your armor then fall into place because you have secured the belt of Truth.

THE BREASTPLATE OF RIGHTEOUSNESS

The breastplate protected the vital organs of the Roman soldier. It covered his body, front and back, from the top of his neck all the way down to his knees. The breastplate was heavy but an excellent defensive piece of weaponry. It was made of metal and was usually covered with many smaller pieces of overlapping metal. The pieces of metal rubbed against each other as the soldier walked and made the breastplate shine brightly. The reflection of the sun could blind an enemy's eyes and send fear through his body as the army approached the battle. It was a formidable sight.

When you are wearing your breastplate of righteousness, you are an awesome sight. Visualize the spirit world where the light of God's righteousness blinds the enemy. This covering protects you from the attacks of the devil every bit as much as the Roman soldier's vital organs were guarded by his breastplate. Righteousness, right standing with God, shields you from grenades of doubt and fear. You are the righteousness of God in Christ Jesus if you have accepted Jesus as your personal Savior. You do not have to earn it. It is a free gift. It is issued to you just like present-day soldiers are given all the gear they need before entering training. Put on your breastplate and walk in confidence, for you, Mighty Warrior, are covered by almighty God.

Living in the righteousness of God is a strategic weapon for battle. It is your defense against those thoughts that Satan uses to torment you. Think of it as psychological warfare. The devil's goal is to destroy you from within, prevent you from walking in your rightful place in Christ. Use your breastplate of righteousness effectively. Know who you are. Let the lies of your enemy bounce off your breastplate. For it to be strong, you must reinforce it daily. Remember, a soldier trains daily for battle. The physical drills of calisthenics and the study of war plans keep him alert and in top shape to be ready for duty at a moment's notice. That's the same requirement for you. Study God's promises about your righteousness and what He says about you. The Truth is your greatest weapon. Memorize scripture so you can use those Words to bludgeon the enemy. Bathe yourself in The Word so that your entire body is protected by your breastplate of righteousness. Then your shining armor blinds the devil from whatever angle he attacks.

THE SHOES OF PEACE

If you are a runner or hiker, you know how important a good pair of shoes is. Combat boots are the foundation for a warrior. The last thing you want to deal with when attacking or evading the enemy is bloody blisters on your feet brought on by ill-fitting shoes. The Roman soldier paid close attention to his boots. They were made of thick leather and covered the feet and shins with laces going up the calves. His boots protected his feet and shins from injury from his opponents. One of the tactics of Roman soldiers was to kick the enemy to the ground so that he could not fight back. That maneuver often

What If? Freedom Ministries ~ P.O. Box 470252 ~ Tulsa, Oklahoma 74147-0252 ~ 918-249-FREE (3733) ~ www.whatifministires.com

107

meant the death of the soldier. Staying on his feet was paramount to victory. To help do that, the soles of his boots were covered with nails similar to cleats on athletic shoes today designed to give the soldier sure footing and proper stance in battle. The nails had a two-fold purpose, to provide stability and to be an offensive weapon for stomping on the enemy.

Your feet shod with the gospel of peace are both offensive and defensive weapons. Just like a good pair of sneakers helps you in sports or just every day walking, your shoes of peace are a foundational part of your armor. They protect you in battle when you are going through the tough times in your life. There is nothing that feels better than a comfortable, well-worn pair of shoes. You need to be comfortable and familiar with the peace of Jesus Christ to battle to your utmost ability. Study the scriptures to know the peace that is yours for the asking. Those shoes of peace are meant to keep you calm and peaceful so you can hear God's voice at all times and put your enemies under your feet.

A warrior entering battle must be able to focus on the task at hand – defeating the enemy. If he is worried and troubled, he cannot give 100%. Trust the peace that Jesus gives you, that peace that passes understanding. In that peace He directs your steps and helps you face the challenges of each day. You are then able to conquer every attack and temptation. Remember the nails on the soles of the Roman soldier's boots? They anchored the soldier to the ground so that he could fight the enemy from a place of strength. Jesus is your firm foundation and anchors you in The Word so that you can stand tall in battle.

The devil has no power over you when you are in that place of peace. His lies, threats, and taunts cannot knock you down when you plant your feet on Christ's peace. The Bible declares in Romans 16:20 (MSG) "The God of peace will come down on Satan with both feet, stomping him into the dirt." Those boots of peace defeat the adversary every time. God uses your feet along with His peace to fight this war. You do not fight alone. The sound of a mighty army is a tremendous sound. A large army can make the ground tremble (and the enemy too) when they march in unison into battle. Think about the sound those spikes on the soles of the Roman soldiers' boots must have made. Frightening! With your shoes of peace and your buddies working together in battle, you trample the devil when he tries to divert you. Do not give any ground to the enemy. Do not listen to his lies. March forward right over the obstacles in your path. Stomp on the devil. Crush his head with your boots. Destroy his hold over you and march to victory.

SHIELD OF FAITH

The ancient Roman shield protected the soldier from the attacks and arrows of the opponent. The battle shield was big enough to hide the soldier's entire body from danger. It was made of thick wood or several layers of animal hides woven together. It was tough and durable. The warrior maintained his shield carefully, oiling it to keep it strong and supple. Without oiling, the shield would crack and be worthless in battle. In addition to the oil, the shield was also soaked in water. One of the deadliest weapons in Roman times was fiery arrows. They contained fluids that burst into flame upon impact.

What If? Freedom Ministries ~ P.O. Box 470252 ~ Tulsa, Oklahoma 74147-0252 ~ 918-249-FREE (3733) ~ www.whatifministires.com

108

Without the shield being soaked in water, the flames would consume the shield and leave the soldier at the mercy of his enemy. Without the aid of the water-soaked shields to douse the fires, fortifications that could not be breached by the army might be destroyed from the flaming arrows.

Your shield of faith is vital to your survival. Attached to your belt of Truth, your shield covers your entire body just like the Roman shield. Maintenance of your shield requires daily diligence. Oil, the anointing of the Holy Spirit, helps you not to crack under the pressure of intense battle. Walking in the anointing strengthens your faith. The water of the Word protects you further from enemy attack. Scripture says to take the shield of faith with which you will be able to quench all the fiery darts of the wicked one. Satan aims his fiery darts at you. He may try to burn a hole into your emotions causing you to react to situations in anger, hatred, lust, doubt, or worry. A little spark can ignite a huge fire. Live your life grounded in The Word so that the darts cannot consume you. Daily oil your shield by following the leading of the Holy Spirit and saturate it with the water of The Word. Only then can you quench the fiery darts of the wicked one.

Faith comes by hearing, and hearing by The Word. Once again a major part of your training involves studying The Word of God. 2 Timothy 2:15 (AMP) states, "Study and be eager and do your utmost to present yourself to God approved (tested by trial), a workman who has no cause to be ashamed, correctly analyzing and accurately dividing (rightly handling and skillfully teaching) the Word of Truth." A true warrior takes pride in his ability as a soldier. He trains constantly to avoid appearing weak or unprepared when it is time to fight. Every day you face obstacles and opportunities to grow. Embrace your trials and learn from each challenge so that your faith is a living part of you. God has given you all the faith you need to fight heroically. Firmly grasp your shield of faith and hold it proudly.

HELMET OF SALVATION

Roman helmets were usually made of bronze. The main shape was that of a bowl to cover the soldier's head. Added to that was a neck guard on the back to protect him from blows to the back of his head and neck. Cheek pieces guarded the sides of his face. The front of the helmet came down low over his forehead to shield him from blows to his face. The inside was cushioned for additional protection and to make it more comfortable to wear since it was worn at all times. It was another heavy piece of armor with multiple functions. In addition to protecting the soldier's head, the helmet was often covered with etchings and plumes of beautiful colors. Functional yet beautiful, the helmet was the soldier's crowning glory.

Your helmet of salvation is an even greater crowning glory for you. It comes right from the throne of heaven. Jesus Christ shed his blood and died to purchase your salvation. It is priceless. And it is functional. The helmet of salvation protects your head just as the Roman soldier's helmet guarded his. In this spiritual war, your mind is particularly vulnerable to attack from the enemy. Remember, the battle is for your mind. The devil will assault you from all sides to convince you that you are defeated. He comes to steal,

What If? Freedom Ministries ~ P.O. Box 470252 ~ Tulsa, Oklahoma 74147-0252 ~ 918-249-FREE (3733) ~ www.whatifministires.com

109

kill, and destroy all that Jesus bought at Calvary. Some of those treasures that are yours include love, joy, peace, healing, purity, a sound mind, righteousness, and so much more. Mighty Warrior, study your training manual so that there is no doubt about who you are in Christ and what belongs to you. Satan tries to capture your territory one battle at a time. You do not have to give him one inch. He has no power or authority over you. But your enemy is tricky. If he sees a crack in your helmet, he will make a wedge to widen the gap. You must keep your helmet sealed with The Word of God. There it is again. Study the Scriptures. That belt of Truth, The Word, holds all your armor together. The more you reinforce your mind with Truth, the less power Satan has over you. When you recognize the devil's lies and repel them with His Word, you win.

SWORD OF THE SPIRIT, THE WORD OF GOD

The final complement to the Roman soldier's armor was his sword. It was long, pointed, and sharp on both sides. This two-edged sword inflicted great damage on its intended victim. It had somewhat jagged edges and a tip that turned slightly upward. This weapon not only pierced the victim's body going in but also could rip his organs to pieces with the flick of a wrist. The sword was a deadly weapon when used skillfully.

Your Sword of the Spirit is an amazingly powerful weapon that can kill your enemy instantly. In Revelation 1:16, Jesus is depicted as having a two-edged sword coming out of His mouth. The Word of God is like a two-edged sword at your disposal. A man of honor studies The Word so that scriptures are a part of his arsenal, ready at all times. Train and practice listening to the voice of the Holy Spirit. That way, when a surprise attack heads your way, you are prepared to speak Truth like the Roman soldier skewered his enemy with his sword.

Scripture spoken out loud kills the devil's plan for you. He is the prince of the air; the atmosphere is his territory. Speaking proper words is like launching missiles that travel far and last forever. When God created the world, He spoke it into existence. His words are just as powerful coming from your mouth. It is important to speak The Word out loud so that God's power has full effect. You cannot see the Words; but just like the wind, they are there. You can absolutely see the effects of spoken scripture just like you can see the results of a tornado tearing through a town. Train yourself to see into the spirit world and seek God's eternal perspective.

Do not underestimate the power of your words. Proverbs 18:21 says the tongue has the power of life and death. Be careful. That power works both ways. By speaking the lies of the devil, you give authority to his plans. If he plants the idea in your mind that you are all alone and cannot take a stand for righteousness, shout The Word. Speak life over your trials and temptations. If I walk through the valley of the shadow of death, I won't fear evil; for God is with me. (Psalm 23) If you feel like you cannot go on one more day, yell that God has not given you more than you can handle, but He always provides a way of escape. (1 Corinthians 10:13) Study The Bible and memorize verses that address your particular areas of weakness. Understand that God has provided a bonus for you if you study The Word. In John 14:26 Jesus promised that the Holy Spirit would bring to

What If? Freedom Ministries ~ P.O. Box 470252 ~ Tulsa, Oklahoma 74147-0252 ~ 918-249-FREE (3733) ~ www.whatifministires.com

110

your remembrance what He spoke to your heart. That is one very important reason why you should study and memorize scriptures. Isn't it great to recognize that God Himself will trigger previous teaching as needed? Data in; data out. You put verses in your mind and spirit by studying/training. The Holy Spirit's job is to fire those shots when you are in the midst of battle. The Holy Spirit is your secret weapon. Allow Him to control your mind, will, and emotions.

PRAYER

You, Mighty Warrior, have one piece of armor that the Roman soldier did not. You have the privilege of praying. This tool is indispensable. Prayer is a pre-emptive strike against the enemy. Prayer gives you strength. Prayer provides wisdom and discernment. Prayer keeps you in touch with your heavenly Father. Without prayer, you are weak and easily defeated. Another of the devil's tactics is to keep you from praying. He presents interruptions like sleepiness, phone calls, noises, and the urge to go to the bathroom to distract you from the task at hand. You may be too busy or lazy. The phone might ring just as you begin to connect with God. Resist the distractions and pray. Pray as if your very life depends on it. It does. You do not have to be fancy or use King James language when you pray. Talk to God. Complain to Him. Be honest with Him. Listen to Him. Communicate as you would with your best friend. He is more than your best Friend. Discipline yourself to pray at all times, about all things. God cares about the big and the little issues of your life. Share all your concerns, joys, frustrations, victories with Him. Prayer should be a very automatic response throughout your day. It is important to have a set-aside time to pray each day; but also develop an attitude of praying all day about all things. Then you can walk immersed in the Holy Spirit, protected on every side from your adversary.

Ephesians 6:10-18 in The Message Bible offers a unique translation that sums up how you should use the armor God has provided for you.

> And that about wraps it up. God is strong, and He wants you strong.
> So take everything the Master has set out for you, well-made weapons
> of the best materials. And put them to use so you will be able to stand
> up to everything the devil throws your way. This is no afternoon
> athletic contest that we'll walk away from and forget about in a couple of
> hours. This is for keeps, a life-or-death fight to the finish against the devil
> and all his angels. Be prepared. You're up against far more than you can
> handle on your own. Take all the help you can get, every weapon God has
> issued, so that when it's all over but the shouting, you'll still be on your
> feet. Truth, righteousness, peace, faith, and salvation are more than words.
> Learn how to apply them. You'll need them throughout your life. God's
> Word is an indispensable weapon. In the same way, prayer is essential in
> this ongoing warfare. Pray hard and long. Pray for your brothers and sisters.
> Keep each other's spirits up so that no one falls behind or drops out.

What If? Freedom Ministries ~ P.O. Box 470252 ~ Tulsa, Oklahoma 74147-0252 ~ 918-249-FREE (3733) ~ www.whatifministires.com

111

Study the following scriptures to reinforce this teaching on God's armor.

Isaiah 51:7-8

_____

_____

Isaiah 54:17

_____

_____

John 14:26-27

_____

_____

Romans 10:17

_____

_____

Romans 13:14

_____

_____

Colossians 3:15

_____

_____

What If? Freedom Ministries ~ P.O. Box 470252 ~ Tulsa, Oklahoma 74147-0252 ~ 918-249-FREE (3733) ~ www.whatifministires.com

112

Hebrews 4:12

_____

_____

Memory verse – 2 Corinthians 10:4-5 (NIV)

The weapons we fight with are not the weapons of the world. On the contrary, they have divine power to demolish strongholds. We demolish arguments and every pretension that sets itself up against the knowledge of God, and we take captive every thought to make it obedient to Christ.

Thinking Points

Describe two ways that you can use the belt of Truth in your daily life.

_____

_____

_____

Describe two ways that you can use your breastplate of righteousness.

_____

_____

_____

What are two ways you can use your shoes of peace in your war for excellence?

_____

_____

_____

What If? Freedom Ministries ~ P.O. Box 470252 ~ Tulsa, Oklahoma 74147-0252 ~ 918-249-FREE (3733) ~ www.whatifministires.com

113

How have you used your shield of faith to protect you from the enemy?

_____

_____

_____

Describe two ways your helmet of salvation has protected your mind from evil.

_____

_____

_____

How do you use the Sword of the Spirit (The Word of God) to fight your battle for integrity?

_____

_____

_____

Do you have a specific time to pray daily? When and where? If not, pick a time and place and write it down here. Date this as a commitment to spend quality time with God every day. (Start with just five minutes if need be, but start.)

_____

_____

_____

What If?
God has provided your weapons and armor for the real war in the spirit world so you can thrive now in the physical world.

What If? Freedom Ministries ~ P.O. Box 470252 ~ Tulsa, Oklahoma 74147-0252 ~ 918-249-FREE (3733) ~ www.whatifministires.com

Chapter 12
Covenant Warrior

You were made to be a Warrior. But it's time to add an additional word. You were made to be a COVENANT Warrior. Yes, if you believe in The Bible and Jesus Christ, the Son of the living God, YOU ARE A COVENANT MAN. You have all the rights and privileges that go along with the covenant. You do not have to be a Mighty Warrior by yourself. In fact, if you try to fight this war by yourself, you will fail. Why would anyone want to fight alone when he has all the power and resources of God Almighty, the Creator of the universe, at his disposal? Your heavenly Father made a covenant to give you all that you need before you were born.

What is a covenant? Why should you be interested in it? How can being in a covenant relationship help you fight your war for excellence? Most Christians do not understand what a covenant is much less why it is invaluable in their every day lives. This chapter will give you a mini-course about a covenant life and the importance of being a Covenant Warrior.

Many think a covenant is the same thing as a contract. The two are similar, yet different. Both are agreements between two or more people in which each party promises to do something or provide a specific item. In our culture covenant is not a popular idea. People prefer a contract that implies an "if you do your part, I'll do my part" mentality. If one of the parties does not fulfill his obligation, the contract is considered broken, void. Many contracts contain loopholes to provide a way of escape if one or more parties do not like the way things are progressing. A biblical covenant is also an agreement between two or more people or nations, but it goes beyond the contract terms. God's covenants are eternal and irrevocable. They are unconditional. The other person doing his part does not determine if the agreement will be honored. God never breaks a covenant.

When Jesus died on the cross to save you from your sins, you were guaranteed the privilege of believing in Him and being forgiven of every possible sin – no matter what. To receive the benefits of this covenant, you do have to do your part. Asking Jesus to be your Savior and receiving Him into your life is step one. That's how you become a covenant man. Walking in covenant brings an entirely new dimension into your life. You die to your old life when you enter the new life God gives you. Covenant is not to be taken lightly. This is a serious agreement between you and God, a lifelong bond paid for by the blood of Jesus. Although God's love is unconditional, you are expected to fulfill your part of the covenant by obeying Him in every aspect of your life. You obey because you love your Abba Father. If you fail, you repent and keep on going. You are not perfect, but you do not <u>habitually</u> sin when you walk in covenant. (1 John 3:4-9)

For example, repeatedly sinning and violating the covenant relationship created all kinds of problems for the Israelites. That is the main reason they spent 40 years in the wilderness after leaving Egypt. They witnessed one miracle after another as Jehovah

What If? Freedom Ministries ~ P.O. Box 470252 ~ Tulsa, Oklahoma 74147-0252 ~ 918-249-FREE (3733) ~ www.whatifministires.com

115

God delivered them from the bondage of the Egyptians. During the journey to the Promised Land, which was part of their covenant promise, God continued to perform miracles and provide for every need. The Israelites walked in unbelief, were ungrateful, murmured, and complained at every obstacle. They built idols and often did things "their way" instead of following God's direction. They struggled in disobedience and suffered incredibly for poor choices. Yet, God never stopped loving them nor did He break His covenant with them. However, His protection and blessings were removed as a judgment against the Israelites for their disobedience and unbelief. God is full of mercy and grace; but with continual sin in a person or nation, He will remove His hand of protection to nudge them back into covenant behavior. Take your covenant seriously.

God is a God of covenant, and The Bible is a book full of covenants. Everything that is important to God involves covenant. God made a covenant with Noah that He would protect his family and never again destroy the Earth with water. The sign of that agreement was the rainbow. God made a covenant with Abraham, gave him the land of Israel, and promised him that his descendants would outnumber the stars and bless the world. Out of Abraham's seed, the Jewish nation and Jesus were born. God made a covenant with David that his Descendant would rule the world from Jerusalem. Jesus, born into the lineage of King David, will reign from the Holy City when He returns to Earth to rule forever. Those are only three of many covenants in The Bible.

Let's take a closer look at biblical covenant to help you understand the importance of this topic. The Bible is divided into two sections, the Old Testament and the New Testament. Testament is another word for covenant. The old covenant is the basis for the new; the new completes God's covenant with the human race. From the time Adam and Eve sinned in the garden, God began His plan to save people from their sin and reconcile them to relationship with Him. With Noah, God preserved his family through the ridicule of the ark-building phase and then protected them during the destruction of the Earth by the flood. God did not have to do that, but He chose to make that covenant with Noah. God offers the same covenant to you. He wants to preserve you from ridicule and peer pressure and protect you during your storms of life. His ark of protection is available to you whenever you need it. Just like he gave humanity a fresh start after the flood, he offers you a new life as you walk in covenant with Him. Remember that every time you see a rainbow in the sky. That is one of your Father's signs of covenant with you.

God picked another common, ordinary man, Abram, for a covenant relationship with Him. (Genesis 12:1-3) His first stipulation was that Abram leave the comfort of his family and country to go where God would show him. Abram was challenged to obey without question or understanding. And obey he did. Once again, God Almighty initiated a covenant relationship with a mere mortal that deserved nothing. But God, in His wisdom and goodness, offered Abram a deal he couldn't refuse. God still gives Himself in covenant relationships with us humans even though we don't deserve it and He doesn't have to give it. You are every bit as special to Jehovah God as Abram was.

You can read about the covenant with Abram in Genesis 17. God not only promised to give Abram the land of Canaan, the Promised Land, but also to make him the father of

What If? Freedom Ministries ~ P.O. Box 470252 ~ Tulsa, Oklahoma 74147-0252 ~ 918-249-FREE (3733) ~ www.whatifministires.com

116

many nations through a child to be born to him and his wife Sarai. Understand that Abram and Sarai were both in their 90's at the time, so this would be quite an accomplishment. But God does what He says He will do. Abram's part was to walk and live blamelessly before God. In other words, Abram was to obey God's commands. If he did, God would make him the father of many nations; bless him spiritually and materially; and make his name great. After this time, his name changed to Abraham which means father of a multitude. God honored His word, the covenant, and gave Abram the land of promise; it was fertile and made him prosperous. And in their old age, Abraham and Sarah became the parents of the miracle child Isaac. Had Abraham chosen not to obey, God would have continued to maintain the covenant relationship, but Abraham would have missed out on the blessings that were the result of the covenant. Abraham obeyed God and walked in the blessing of this biblical covenant the rest of his life.

The promises to Abraham were foundational to God's covenant with all of us today. This was a type of foreshadowing of Jesus fulfilling the covenant to save the world. God tested Abraham's commitment to Him by asking him to sacrifice his only son, Isaac, on an altar. Without question, Abraham obeyed God and prepared for the sacrifice. He went as far as placing Isaac on the altar and raising his knife to give his only son back to God. At this point, God stopped Abraham and provided a ram as a substitute for Isaac. The intent of this exercise was never to kill Isaac but to test Abraham. He proved that he trusted God enough to give up his only son who had been born to fulfill the promise of the covenant. This paved the way for the fulfillment of God's promise according to Genesis 22:16-18, the provision of his Seed, God's only Son Jesus Christ, to bring salvation to the world. That is something worth shouting about.

With the foundation of covenant in place throughout the Old Testament, the birth of Jesus begins the fulfillment of the blessing in the New Testament. Stop a moment and think about the significance of the birth of Jesus. His only purpose for being born was so He could die. He left the majesty and glory of heaven to complete the promise of God to provide the way to relationship with Him. No more animal sacrifices, Jesus paid the debt once and for all. He knew people would reject Him, make fun of Him, betray Him, ridicule Him, disrespect Him, beat Him to within an inch of His life, and eventually kill Him in one of the most painful and humiliating ways possible. Yet, Jesus agreed to this life willingly – **for you**. **Wow!** The covenant that began with Abraham and the twelve tribes of Israel culminated in the death of Jesus, your substitute for the penalties of your sins. Jesus then inherited the promises of the Old Testament covenant between Abraham and God. Abraham did become the father of many nations, walk in spiritual and material blessings, and his name is even today famous. Jesus reigns in heaven now and will one day rule physically over all the nations of the world. He provides riches beyond imagination both spiritually and materially for you. His name is exalted above all else.

God's covenants are binding and eternal. He cannot go against His Word and must honor His promises. A Covenant Warrior also respects his word. It is apparent how important covenant is to God and every believer. But a few more points here will help explain the workings of covenant in your life. God is always the initiator and superior party in

What If? Freedom Ministries ~ P.O. Box 470252 ~ Tulsa, Oklahoma 74147-0252 ~ 918-249-FREE (3733) ~ www.whatifministires.ccm

117

biblical covenant, and He determines the terms of the covenant. He chooses you to be in covenant with Him. His promises are unconditional. Yet, you must do your part as a participant in the covenant. It may be difficult to understand how God's love can be unconditional yet require action on your part. Our society tends to define "unconditional" as getting anything you want whenever you want it. That is not God's definition of "unconditional." His unconditional love is eternal and binding. God will always love you even when you break your promises to Him. Covenant is not based on how you respond to the conditions of it. It depends completely on God's grace and will. But you have a part to play in how you live your life and walk before Him. You have to follow the terms of the covenant to receive the blessings prepared for you. Every choice has consequences for good or bad. Abraham chose to obey even to the point of giving up his son. The covenant did not depend on Abraham's obedience but on God's grace and mercy. The blessings came **after** obedience to the terms of the covenant. You, too, must choose to obey just as every good soldier obeys orders. Soldiers follow a great leader out of respect and loyalty, not fear. You, too, should not obey out of fear but out of love for Abba Father. John 14:15 (AMP) says, "If you (really) love Me, you will keep (obey) My commands."

Living a covenant life involves your total commitment to your Commander-in-Chief. You trust Him to have only your best interests at heart even if you do not understand what He is requiring of you. You obey out of love and faith in the One Who is faithful. You have a covenant Partner to consider in every choice you make. Dying to self, giving up what you want for the benefit of your Partner, becomes your lifestyle. In light of covenant, what Paul wrote in Galatians 2:20 (NIV) takes on a new and deeper meaning. "I have been crucified with Christ and I no longer live, but Christ lives in me. The life I live in the body, I live by faith in the Son of God, who loved me and gave himself for me."

If you do not obey, does that mean that God no longer loves you and voids the contract? Absolutely not! God can never break His Word. God never rejects or abandons you. He remains with you always. Because Jesus walked on Earth as a human, He understands and sympathizes with your trials of daily life. He never condemns you but convicts you of wrongdoing. But disobedience, in a way, ties His hands so He cannot help you the way He wants. His commitment to you is unconditional and available at all times, but you may experience God's punishment as a result of disobedience. Hebrews 12:5-11 (NIV) explains the Lord's discipline for you, His son.

> My son, do not make light of the Lord's discipline, and do
> not lose heart when He rebukes you, because the Lord
> disciplines those He loves, and He punishes everyone he
> accepts as a son. Endure hardship as discipline; God is
> treating you as sons. For what son is not disciplined by
> his father? If you are not disciplined (and everyone
> undergoes discipline), then you are illegitimate children
> and not true sons. Moreover, we have all had human fathers
> who disciplined us and we respected them for it. How much

What If? Freedom Ministries ~ P.O. Box 470252 ~ Tulsa, Oklahoma 74147-0252 ~ 918-249-FREE (3733) ~ www.whatifministires.com

118

more should we submit to the Father of our spirits and live!
Our fathers disciplined us for a little while as they thought
best; but God disciplines us for our good, that we may share
in his holiness. No discipline seems pleasant at the time, but
painful. Later on, however, it produces a harvest of righteousness
and peace for those who have been trained by it.

Take your covenant relationship seriously. God initiated it because He loves you and desires to walk with you every step of your life. Those who walk in covenant are blessed. You are blessed so that you can bless others. That's the full cycle of covenant. God initiates a relationship with you. You accept the terms of the agreement and walk in obedience. Out of that come blessings. You pass on your blessings to others which blesses your Father. He showers you with more blessings.

The story of David and Jonathan in First and Second Samuel is a beautiful account of a relationship that may help you understand covenant even better. Jonathan was King Saul's son, the next in line to the throne. He and David became dear friends and made a covenant to seal their commitment to each other. In 1 Samuel 18: 4 as part of the agreement Jonathan gave David his robe, armor, sword, bow, and belt. That may seem strange to you in today's society, but in their culture that was extremely significant. By giving David his robe, Jonathan was saying that David was not alone but covered by Jonathan (his robe). He put himself on David. Jonathan's gift of his armor meant that now David's enemies were also Jonathan's and vice versa. They would fight for each other and protect each other at all costs, even to death. Remember the belt on the Roman soldiers' armor? Jonathan gave David his belt that held everything together. It signified his strength being available for David whenever needed to hold everything together in the day-to-day battle of life. This relationship took precedence over all others, even family. When King Saul was determined to kill David, Jonathan, the king's own son, is the one who warned David to flee for his life. There was one other aspect to this covenant that is significant here. Jonathan and David agreed that their covenant would carry over to future generations.

There are great similarities between David and Jonathan's covenant and God's covenant with you. The Bible instructs you to put on Jesus, the robe of righteousness that covers you from danger. You are not alone in your battles, because Jesus covers you with His robe. As you studied in the last chapter, God has given you a whole set of armor to use in your daily battles in life. He is fighting with you and gives you the strength and stamina to conquer every enemy. He never leaves you. God's belt of Truth holds you together when the devil tries to confuse you and lead you into his traps to destroy you. Your enemies are God's enemies, and God's enemies are yours. God defends you and stands up for you. Likewise, you must stand up for and defend righteousness. Let your Father deal with your enemies while you love them and pray for them. Do not be entangled with the distractions of the world. Stay focused on God's battle plan for you. (2 Timothy 2:4) Give your covenant relationship with Jesus priority over every other one. God is over all.

What If? Freedom Ministries ~ P.O. Box 470252 ~ Tulsa, Oklahoma 74147-0252 ~ 918-249-FREE (3733) ~ www.whatifministires.com

119

When Jonathan and David agreed the covenant would extend to their descendants, they probably had no idea where that would lead. After both Saul and Jonathan were killed in the same battle, David became king. Only one remained of Jonathan's family, his young son Mephibosheth. Hearing the news of the deaths of his father and grandfather, the members of Jonathan's household panicked. In her haste to flee the wrath of the new king, Mephibosheth's nanny grabbed the child and ran for their lives. She fell, injuring both of the boy's ankles, crippling him for the rest of his life. The entire household moved to the town of Lo-debar where they lived in barrenness.

Eventually, King David remembered his promise and learned that Jonathan had a son living in Lo-debar. The king summoned Mephibosheth to his court. He responded in fear and panic expecting to be executed by David. In fact, he asked David, "What is your servant that you should look upon such a dead dog as I am?" (2 Samuel 9:8 AMP) David reached out to Jonathan's heir with love and mercy. Mephibosheth thought of himself as a "dead dog" not someone worthy of love from the king. How could that be? Mephibosheth had believed a lie for years. (If you believe a lie, it becomes truth for you.) Because of misinformation and rumors from those around him, he had lived in fear and poverty. He was ignorant of the covenant between his father and the king. But David was an honorable man who took the covenant seriously. Can you imagine the shock when David invited Mephibosheth to eat at the king's table – for the rest of his life? Additionally, the king restored all of his inheritance due him from his father and grandfather. Finally, Mephibosheth could live like the true heir that he had always been.

Can you identify with Mephibosheth? Have you listened to others tell you their opinion of God – He does not care about you; He is a mean and spiteful God? Have you believed lies about your rights as a covenant son of the most-high God? Have you lived in fear dreading what God might do to you as punishment for some sin? Have you believed the lie that if you surrender to His will, you will live in bondage to Him and never have any fun? Has your ignorance about the true nature of God ever kept you crippled and cowering in a corner unable to claim your benefits as the King's child? Have you thought of yourself as a "dead dog" unworthy of love and blessing? Have you run in panic from God and tried to take care of yourself? How many years did Mephibosheth waste in Lo-debar?

Mephibosheth missed out on his inheritance for years because he believed lies. He trusted what others told him about King David but never checked out the facts for himself. He did not KNOW David, his character, or the covenant benefits available to him. Because of prejudice and ignorance, the rightful heir of Jonathan suffered unnecessarily. What about you, Warrior? How well do you KNOW your King? Do you listen to others for information about your heavenly Father and live in the traditions and habits of rumors and prejudice? Have you felt abandoned and unworthy of love when it seemed God didn't care about you or rescue you from a bad situation? Are you living in your own Lo-debar fearing the One Who knows you best and loves you most? Have you been living in ignorance of your covenant? You are covered with the robe of Jesus. Because of His covenant with you, you are worthy to eat at the King's table and receive all the rights and benefits of royalty. Mighty Warrior, do not waste another moment

What If? Freedom Ministries ~ P.O. Box 470252 ~ Tulsa, Oklahoma 74147-0252 ~ 918-249-FREE (3733) ~ www.whatifministires.com

120

believing the enemy's lies! You are a covenant man, an heir of the Lord Jesus Christ. Your covenant means you have all the rights and privileges that Jesus died to give you. Covenant is every bit as important for you today as it was for David and Jonathan.

God is still a covenant God. Your loving Father made a covenant with you, the most important covenant in history, when Jesus died on the cross so that your sins could be forgiven. That blood covenant puts Jesus and His shed blood between you and God. The robe of Jesus covers you. Then God sees only Jesus when He looks at you. Once your sins are forgiven, God can no longer remember them. (Psalm 103:12) He sees you through the righteousness of Jesus Christ. Think of it this way. Put a penny in your hand. The penny represents you. Your hand stands for Jesus and His robe of righteousness. Your eyes looking at the penny and your hand symbolize God. With the penny in the palm of your hand, make a fist. Do you see the penny? No, it is covered by your hand, Jesus. That is how God sees you – Jesus all over you – when you have accepted the blood covenant made on the cross of Calvary. Your sins are forgiven and white as snow because you are covered by His shed blood. This covenant is eternal. God does not change His mind. You can do nothing to force Him to break the covenant. Even if you do not fulfill your part of the agreement, God's covenant is everlasting.

Covenant is good and honorable. Most do not understand the seriousness of covenant and break it without thought. In today's society, many do not honor their word. People agree to something quickly without thinking through the consequences. If the tasks become too difficult or time-consuming, they quit. Satan knows that covenant binds people together and unites them in battle; and he will do everything in his power to divide and conquer. A man of integrity does what he says he will do. Mighty Warrior, it is important that you follow through on your commitments. Loyalty, a type of covenant, is a vital part of a soldier's character. To know you can be trusted makes you stand head and shoulders above the common man and gives you a great advantage in battle.

To be in a covenant relationship with God is an amazing privilege. Some believe that His covenants are a string of "no's." But it is so much more than a list of "do's" and "don'ts." Yet, rules are a big part of covenant. The Ten Commandments are a part of covenant and contain several "shall not's." But, when obeyed, each commandment protects you from dangerous consequences. Your covenant with God protects you in battle. It is an unseen but vital part of your armor. Learn to view it as a positive influence in your life, not a negative.

There are various types of covenant; but let's look at the blood covenant. It is comprised of four steps – a sacrifice and shedding of blood, speaking the contents of the covenant (declaring the details of the agreement to each other), an exchange of names signifying your oneness as part of the covenant, and the covenant meal. In ancient cultures, sharing a meal was a pledge of loyalty to each other. The death of Jesus on the cross is the perfect example of a blood covenant. Jesus sacrificed his life, his blood, on the cross for you and all of mankind, step one. When you accept Jesus as your Savior, you say so publicly (step two – speak the contents of the covenant) and are baptized. Baptism is a symbolic act of your dying to your will and accepting the death of Jesus and His shed

What If? Freedom Ministries ~ P.O. Box 470252 ~ Tulsa, Oklahoma 74147-0252 ~ 918-249-FREE (3733) ~ www.whatifministires.com

121

blood to cover your sins. Step three is an exchange of names. When you accept Jesus as your Savior, you are called a Christian or Christ follower. You are a new person, one with Christ, with a new name. The fourth and last step is the covenant meal. For a believer, taking communion to remember how Jesus suffered and died is an important part of the relationship with God. In a way, the meal seals the covenant.

Marriage is a covenant between a man, a woman, and God. After salvation, this is the most important covenant. Thinking about the seriousness of this promise now, before you consider marriage, will protect you from many pitfalls in the future. Marriage, a blood covenant, follows the four steps also. First, the sacrifice and shedding of blood involve the sacrifice of your will, dying to self. You die to your rights and desires and pledge to put your wife's interests ahead of yours. (If you are not ready to sacrifice your rights, your way of life for your wife, do not proceed to marriage.) If you marry a virgin, the hymen is broken on the wedding night providing the physical blood sacrifice. In the Old Testament, newlyweds had to show proof (the blood-stained sheet) that the woman was a virgin. If they had no proof, the woman could be stoned to death. Sexual intimacy is an act of covenant, a mirror image of the relationship between Jesus and His bride, the church. Second, during the marriage ceremony, the couple exchanges vows; they speak the contents of the covenant. Step three, at the end of the ceremony, the couple is introduced as "Mr. and Mrs." for the first time. They exchange names. The fourth step involves the meal or wedding feast which completes the covenant.

The marriage covenant is a lifelong commitment for better or worse, richer or poorer, in sickness and in health, till death do you part. Giving yourself to a woman is a serious decision. In a society where giving away your virginity is trendy, you must consider your covenant responsibilities. Whenever you are tempted to violate covenant, think about the long-lasting effects of your actions. God intended you to be a one-woman man. If people followed the principles laid out in The Bible regarding relationships and marriage, divorce would not be an epidemic problem today. Pray and seek God's choice for your wife. Put on His robe to protect you in your single life. Embrace the benefits of walking in intimacy with Jesus. You are a covenant man. Act like it.

Let's spend a few minutes discussing what a covenant breaker is. You DO NOT want to be one of those. Most of us are not tempted to murder or steal a million dollars. But you may be tempted to break covenant in other areas that are not as easily recognized. God is interested in the small things, the details of your life. If you use flattery to steal a girl's heart, you break covenant. If you hate any of your classmates, you break covenant. Your word is a covenant. So if you say you will go to a movie with a friend but go with someone else instead, you break covenant. If you tell your parents you will clean up after the dog and don't, you break covenant. If you touch a girl inappropriately, you break covenant. If you lie, you break covenant. If you think you do not need God's help (pride), you break covenant. Get the picture? The little "breaks" impact your life in a big way. Train yourself to be a covenant keeper. The good news is that when you fail, God still maintains covenant with you. Covenant is eternal and binding. Do your part; ask for His forgiveness so that your relationship with Him is restored. Step back into the blessing arena.

What If? Freedom Ministries ~ P.O. Box 470252 ~ Tulsa, Oklahoma 74147-0252 ~ 918-249-FREE (3733) ~ www.whatifministires.com

122

Don't get the idea that being a covenant man forces you to live in a world of "no's." That is the farthest thing from the Truth. Covenant provides hope so you can enjoy life and live in true freedom. Focus on the benefits rather than what you can't do. As a believer in Jesus Christ, you receive all the rights and privileges of the covenant. The slogan, "membership has its privileges," takes on a whole new meaning when you consider covenant with God. First and foremost, you receive salvation and forgiveness of sin. An added benefit is no fear of death but anticipation of eternal life and the promise of heaven. You live under God's grace and mercy instead of legalism. You enjoy the peace that passes all understanding, and have access to healing of all diseases. All shame and fear of rejection have been taken away. You have complete access to your Father God any time and place you want. God goes to war for you and crushes your enemies. You have power over Satan and all the forces of hell. The miracle-working power of God is yours, Covenant Warrior. All of this is yours because of the covenant between you and God.

So, are you up to the challenge? First, if you have never made a serious commitment to Jesus Christ, you need to take care of that right now. Do you believe the following:

- Jesus is the Son of God.
- He came to Earth to die as the Sacrifice for your sins.
- He was killed on the cross at Calvary, was buried, and rose again after three days.
- He went back to heaven and is seated at the right hand of His Father.
- He will return to Earth one day to reign and rule forever.

If you answer yes to each of those questions, then tell God you believe in Jesus and want Him to be your Savior. Ask Him to forgive you of your sins (name any that come to mind). Receive His forgiveness. You are now a son of God. It's that simple. Next, you need to go public. Tell someone about your decision. God initiated this covenant by sending Jesus to Earth. Your part is to believe and receive His love. Remember that covenant relationship involves obligations on your part, obedience. Study your Bible, find a Bible-teaching church, and surround yourself with followers of Christ. Obey God's Word. God is not looking for perfection but progress toward becoming more like Him. The fruits of the Spirit are now available to you. Love, joy, peace, patience, kindness, goodness, faithfulness, gentleness, and self-control (Galatians 5:22) are yours now and are life-changing. And that is just the beginning of the benefits of His covenant with you. Enjoy a close relationship with Abba Father.

If you are already a Christ follower, right now would be a good time to renew your commitment to your Father God. Just as His mercies are new every morning, your love and gratitude should be expressed every day. Mighty Warrior, you are a soldier in God's army. You have the greatest Commander-in-Chief in all of history. And He chose you to enlist in His Army. Accept that honor with happiness and sincerity. The work is hard. The pain can be excruciating. The enemy is on every side. But God surrounds you with His presence and power. You cannot fail! You may lose some battles, but you can win the war. Never forget that. God has given you all the tools, strategies, and support that you need. Train. Exercise physically, mentally, and spiritually. Eat right both physically

What If? Freedom Ministries ~ P.O. Box 470252 ~ Tulsa, Oklahoma 74147-0252 ~ 918-249-FREE (3733) ~ www.whatifministires.com

123

and spiritually. Rest in Him. Study your war manual until it becomes an automatic part of you. Just like Jesus said He and His Father are One, you are to be One with Them. That is the way to enter the battle and defeat every enemy. The battle belongs to the Lord!

Write your thoughts about the following verses and how they relate to your covenant.

Genesis 17:7-11

_____

_____

Exodus 19:4-6

_____

_____

Deuteronomy 7:6-9

_____

_____

Deuteronomy 30:15-16, 19-20

_____

_____

Job 31:1

_____

_____

What If? Freedom Ministries ~ P.O. Box 470252 ~ Tulsa, Oklahoma 74147-0252 ~ 918-249-FREE (3733) ~ www.whatifministires.com

124

Psalm 25:10

_____

_____

Psalm 89:3-4

_____

_____

Luke 1:68-75

_____

_____

John 15:9-17

_____

_____

John 17:15-23 (Jesus' prayer for you)

_____

_____

Galatians 3:28-29

_____

_____

What If? Freedom Ministries ~ P.O. Box 470252 ~ Tulsa, Oklahoma 74147-0252 ~ 918-249-FREE (3733) ~ www.whatifministires.com

125

Colossians 3:9-12

_____

_____

Memory Verse – Deuteronomy 7:9 (NIV)

Know therefore that the Lord your God is God; he is the faithful God, keeping his covenant of love to a thousand generations of those who love him and keep his commands.

Thinking Points

What does "Covenant Warrior" mean to you?

_____

_____

_____

Are there little covenant breakers in your life? What are they? What will you do to avoid breaking covenant?

_____

_____

_____

Are you living in Lo-debar, eating at the King's table, or existing somewhere in between? Explain your answer.

_____

_____

_____

What If? Freedom Ministries ~ P.O. Box 470252 ~ Tulsa, Oklahoma 74147-0252 ~ 918-249-FREE (3733) ~ www.whatifministires.com

126

Did the discussion about the marriage covenant change your way of thinking toward girls? How?

_____

_____

_____

What benefits of walking in covenant do you want to increase in your life? Write three steps you will take toward that goal.

_____

_____

_____

What If?
God trusts you enough to want to be in a covenant relationship with you right now, where you are, and just the way you are.

What If? Freedom Ministries ~ P.O. Box 470252 ~ Tulsa, Oklahoma 74147-0252 ~ 918-249-FREE (3733) ~ www.whatifministires.com

127

Write your own covenant with God regarding integrity and sexual purity. Sign and date it.

_____

_____

_____

_____

_____

_____

_____

_____

_____

_____

_____

_____

_____

_____   _____
Signature   Date

What If? Freedom Ministries ~ P.O. Box 470252 ~ Tulsa, Oklahoma 74147-0252 ~ 918-249-FREE (3733) ~ www.whatifministires.com

128

Congratulations, Mighty Warrior. You have completed basic training. But this is only the beginning. After boot camp, soldiers graduate to advanced training. Your war for integrity is a lifelong one that requires daily maintenance. You have put much time and effort into this first phase. Now you need to continue your training to keep your skills sharp. What you learned while studying Made To Be a Warrior must become an automatic part of you if you are to win. Your adversary is a patient foe and will never give up trying to find ways to trick you and separate you from your Commander-in-Chief. Remember, NOTHING can separate you from the love of God. The battle for your mind is raging in the spirit world. Keep your eyes focused on Jesus and His eternal perspective.

We commission you now, in the name of Jesus Christ, the Son of the living God, to go out with courage. You were created for this purpose. Now assume your position of the Mighty Covenant Warrior that you are. As God was with Moses, Abraham, Daniel, and David, so is He with you. Do not fear. Go forward with God's strength and power. Walk in humility before your God and trust Him to fight alongside you.

> Fight the good fight of the faith. Take hold of the eternal life
> to which you were called when you made your good confession
> in the presence of many witnesses.
> 1 Timothy 6:12 (NIV)

We are praying for you, Mighty Warrior. Never give up. You were **MADE TO WIN**!

What If? Freedom Ministries ~ P.O. Box 470252 ~ Tulsa, Oklahoma 74147-0252 ~ 918-249-FREE (3733) ~ www.whatifministires.com

129

EXTRA RESOURCES

Battle Field of the Mind for Teens by Joyce Meyer

Every Young Man's Battle by Stephen Arterburn and Fred Stoeker

Before You Live Together by David Gudgel

Boundaries by Dr. Henry Cloud and Dr. John Townsend

Boundaries in Dating by Dr. Henry Cloud and Dr. John Townsend

Dateable by Justin Lookadoo and Hayley DiMarco

The Dirt on Sex by Justin Lookadoo

The War Within by Robert Daniels

Who Moved the Goalpost? By Bob Gresh

Wild at Heart by John Eldredge

Websites

www.whatifministries.com

www.enough.org

www.PureFreedom.org

www.Godtube.com

Filters

www.TheTVBoss.org

www.monitoringSoftwareReviews.org

What If? Freedom Ministries ~ P.O. Box 470252 ~ Tulsa, Oklahoma 74147-0252 ~ 918-249-FREE (3733) ~ www.whatifministires.com

130

Made in the USA
Middletown, DE
23 March 2023

27517983R00073